THE WEST MENDIP WAY

Cover: Black Rock Drove and Quarry.

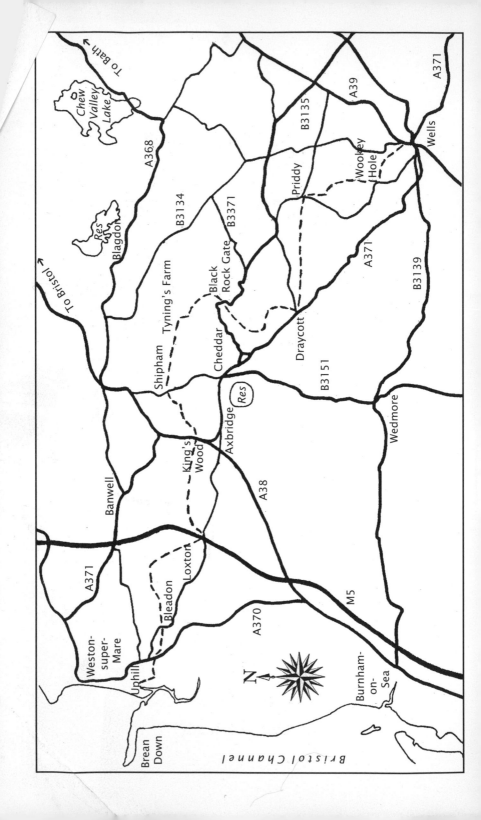

The West Mendip Way

A Guide for Walkers of the
30-mile footpath from
Uphill to Wells

Derek Moyes

EX LIBRIS PRESS

Published in 1999 by
EX LIBRIS PRESS
1 The Shambles
Bradford on Avon
Wiltshire
BA15 1JS

Design and typesetting by
Ex Libris Press

Typeset in 10/13.5 Lucida Bright

Cover printed by
Shires Press, Trowbridge, Wiltshire

Printed in Britain by
Cromwell Press, Trowbridge, Wiltshire

ISBN 0 948578 45 9

Aerial photographs with the kind
assistance of Mr. Ken Stokes

CONTENTS

Using this guidebook

This guide book has two chief functions: to provide a route description to augment existing way-marks, and to describe the many places of interest passed along the way or visible from the path. Of necessity, the two types of description have to be written one within the other. This is fine if there is plenty of time to read them both on the walk, but occasionally, if time is pressing or the weather inclement, you may be concerned primarily with just the direction to take, leaving the rest to be browsed through later.

With this in mind, straightforward route descriptions have been set in italics and highlighted by a shaded box, so that, when necessary, the reader may skip easily to the next section of navigational advice.

Bibliography

Uphill and its Old Church, Lawrence Abram.
The Heart of Mendip, F.A. Knight.
The King's England – Somerset, Arthur Mee.
A Mendip Valley, Theodore Compton.
The Mines of Mendip, J.W. Gough.
Old Mendip, Robin Atthill.
Man and the Mendips, The Mendip Society.
Mendip – A New Study, Edited by Robin Athill.
The Mendips, A. W. Coysh, E. J. Mason & V. Waite.
Mendip Underground, D. Irwin & A. Knibbs.

INTRODUCTION

The beautiful and impressive range of the Mendip Hills in Somerset extends traditionally from Cottle's Oak on Egford Hill, Frome, in the east to the Black Rock, in the estuary of the River Axe, in the west. Geographically, Brean Down and even the island of Steep Holm in the Bristol Channel should also be included.

The hills were known as *Munedep* during the reign of Bishop Joceline Trotman between 1218-1242 and in the patent rolls of Henry III in 1251 it is spelt *Menedep*. The name is possibly a thousand years older than that as it has been suggested that it is an Iron Age reference to mining activities with *Maen* and *Dippa* meaning 'the hill with pits'. Nowadays terms used are the Mendips or, more locally, on Mendip.

The geology of these hills is a very complex and deeply involved subject but basically their great mass consists mainly of Carboniferous or Mountain Limestone fringed with Dolomitic Conglomerate. The highest of the summits are rounded uplands of Old Red Sandstone, generally heather covered as is the highest point, Blackdown, and which receives the most rainfall.

The cracks and faults that have formed in the limestone have been eroded still further by running water to create fissures, caves and gorges, the characteristic features found in any limestone country. In the many valleys and ravines woods have grown to provide a perfect and natural habitat for wildlife. Combining natural history, geography, geology, spelaeology, ancient and industrial history and many other fascinating aspects, the West Mendip Way – with its spectacular views in clear weather from the Mendip plateau – presents a unique opportunity to walk and explore some of the most interesting and outstanding terrain in the West Country.

The Way consists of a series of linked footpaths using public rights of way and was devised and way-marked by the Rotary

Clubs of Weston-super-Mare, Wrington Vale, Mendip and Wells
to commemorate Queen Elizabeth's Silver Jubilee in 1977.

When I first walked the path in the spring of 1982 with my
wife Maria we had been unable to obtain any precise
information, publication or maps relating to it. We set out
with maps that contained outdated information, knowing only
that the general direction was from Uphill, near Weston-super-
Mare to Wells. The notes I scribbled down along the course of
the 30-mile path on various excursions (in all months and all
weathers, travelling both east and west) developed eventually
into this guide book, with its emphasis on non-way-marked
junctions and points of interest along the route.

The Ordnance Survey Explorer series of maps, with a scale
of 1:25,000 (2.5 inches to the mile) are ideal for the walker.
The two that cover the complete route are: Weston-super-Mare
& Bleadon Hill, No.153 and Cheddar George & Mendip Hills
West, No.141. Also very helpful is the Ordnance Survey
Landranger series, Weston-super-Mare & Bridgwater, No.182
with a scale of 1:50,000 (1.25 inches to the mile), covering the
whole route. Older or even antique maps could prove valuable
for the historical or industrial points of interest shown on
them as the modern maps will show less clearly features such
as Roman roads, disused railways or industrial sites. Note that
whatever maps are used, place names, particularly farms, may
change.

I have described the West Mendip Way as walked eastwards,
mainly because there can be no greater finale than the arrival
into Wells, England's smallest, and Somerset's most gracious
city. For the healthy and fit, naturalist and historian, whichever
direction is taken the beauty and splendour of Mendip, with
its abundant wildlife and strong historical associations, is
certain to be pleasurable and satisfying. A map, compass and
binoculars will greatly enhance that pleasure.

This guidebook describes the walk in short sections. In the
maps I have used symbols which should make for easy
identification on the path, particularly when boundaries

consist of walls, hedges or fencing.

The single oak posts used for way-marking has the West Mendip Way marked vertically and generally has a plastic disc set into the post near the top with a white or coloured arrow for direction. When destinations and distances are marked then the arrow is yellow for a public footpath, blue for a bridleway, and red for a public carriage-way. The path is well defined and generally well signposted and I have drawn a symbol for the West Mendip Way posts as they are very helpful, but there is a slight discrepancy between them in the distances they give, especially in the westerly direction.

The West Mendip Way is criss-crossed by so many other footpaths and it is some of these more recently way-marked paths that may be more prominently marked than the route described in this book. Please be aware that the West Mendip Way signposts can decay, become broken or disappear and that also new posts can be erected. Some single discs and other directional signs are also now appearing so it is not always the wooden posts to look for. Now that some other paths have better way-marking please take note of my directions and diagrams.

Trees, hedges, fences, gates, stiles and signposts are not immune from removal, replacement or natural changes, and many of these may appear in new locations originally without them. Temporary diversions around fields may be necessary owing to the growing of crops, and barbed wire may also be encountered. Whilst every endeavour has been made to be as accurate as possible it is likely that further diversions may be made, particularly in the immediate proximity of a farmhouse or farm buildings.

There are now many diversions from the original West Mendip Way but even if the latest official route is not strictly followed this splendid walk through the western and central area of the Mendip Hills can still be covered with a great deal of pleasure. I will emphasise that, despite any diversions, the original route of paths and tracks as known previously are still public rights of way and can be used legally and without any embarrassment or harassment.

The route has now even changed from that which is clearly marked on the two latest 1:25,000 Ordnance Survey maps. Aided by my directions the West Mendip Way can be followed easily and with much enjoyment and satisfaction.

Unlike many other guidebooks or walking articles I have not included walking times. As so much depends on the health and fitness of the walker – and weather conditions, terrain underfoot or a heavy rucksack – so much has to be taken into account. A section of perhaps 3.5 miles (5.6 kms) that can be covered in one hour by one person may take over two hours by someone else just out for a casual stroll and free to relax and appreciate a view where so desired. These glorious hills are not to be hurried but to be enjoyed to the full.

Some suitable car parking has been mentioned in various places but, if not stated, then parking is either impossible or has limitations such as narrow roads in the villages or very restricted verge-side space. Please always park thoughtfully. Overnight accommodation and camping and caravanning sites are mentioned only generally, but details can be obtained in Weston-super-Mare, Wells, or en-route. Permanent and seasonal sites are to be found close to the footpath, and wild camping is also possible providing that the countryside code is respected, landowner's permission granted, and local by-laws are not contravened.

With the ever-changing seasons and climate the natural environment is also liable to change. The wild flowers, plants, shrubs and trees that are in leaf or flower and in abundance in the spring or summer will obviously look somewhat different and may be completely lost to sight in the autumn or winter. Many species of birds or wild animals will have migrated or hibernated until their return again in the spring.

The achievement of successful wildlife and botanical observation and identification is very rewarding and more knowledge is gained in this way than by being informed of the exact position of flowers, birds' nests or badger setts. There is always a danger of accidental disturbance or destruction and so I have not pinpointed the exact locations of, for example, the rare Cheddar pink in Cheddar Gorge or the merlin's nesting place elsewhere along the route. Some butterflies (more than 40 species are known on Mendip) and wild flowers have a short lifecycle and demand acute observation, but botanists, ornithologists and lepidopterists will find much to interest them. Aided by handbooks, the nature lover will find that the subjects that can be studied are almost unlimited.

Agriculture, cheese and cider making, quarrying, paper manufacture, and the mining of lead, iron, coal and other minerals have played a large part in the industrial heritage of the Mendip Hills and have been extremely valuable assets to the communities in the area. Roads and railways have speeded communications and the transportation of goods but since the decline and eventual closure of the railways the evidence of its existence is gradually disappearing.

The research of placenames can be difficult and very time-consuming. Over the centuries, perhaps more than 2000 years, names have been altered out of all recognition from their origination. As historical detail is often incomplete there have been translation errors and so there is now some controversy over the original meanings. Because of this difference of opinion I have therefore given the definition from perhaps more than one source. Many placenames of today still survive from Celtic or Saxon origin. Historical facts, and even well-known legends, are often difficult to determine that which is considered to be the truth as recorded honestly over the centuries and that which is based on hearsay or oral interpretations which is often an unreliable source of information. Legend and folklore are often based on historical fact but because of the lack of undisputed evidence stories are often regarded as fictitious or mythological. Even King Arthur of Camelot and his Knights of the Round Table could probably be classified as this.

During my conversations with the villagers en-route I have learned many ghost stories and mysterious happenings and I have related only briefly a couple or so. I have deliberately avoided using names and other information which might lead to the embarrassment of any relatives still living or even to the present occupiers of the houses concerned. Whispers of murders, suicides and locked rooms have reached my ears and in a couple of cases people have been reluctant to discuss with me the rumours that have circulated and so their wishes and privacy must always be respected.

Concerning walking, remember to wear suitable clothing, taking notice of the weather forecast, and wear stout and firm footwear for some rough and sometimes very muddy terrain. Please heed the countryside code, not only for the benefit of the conservationists, but particularly for the farmers who earn their living from the land and so care and respect for farm property is always appreciated. If heart, lungs and legs are in a fit and healthy condition then others will gain as much satisfaction and pleasure from the West Mendip Way as I have.

In spite of my prolonged research into this project some material has been purposely omitted but further reading is suggested in the bibliography. I, or my publisher, would appreciate any comment or correction that would be regarded as necessary for future reprints, particularly concerning the topographical information offered.

Finally, I acknowledge most sincerely and with many grateful thanks the help, encouragement and assistance that I have received from so many people that it has been my pleasure to meet during my quest for knowledge. I thank most of all my wife Maria, who has shown much patience and understanding during our long walks together and on other occasions when I have been involved with my research. My very grateful thanks also to Mr. Ken Stokes who gave me the opportunity to fly the footpath in both directions to obtain my own aerial photographs by helicopter.

The Start of the West Mendip Way

Uphill, situated almost two miles south of the large and popular seaside resort of Weston-super-Mare, figured much more importantly in the past before Weston's rise to fame. Even the bay was called Uphill Bay on maps drawn in the early 1800's before it was renamed Weston Bay. It was known as *Axium* by the Romans and certain evidence has suggested Roman occupation. Although opinions differ historians agree that the Romans probably did use a harbour to export from Uphill some of the large quantities of lead which they were producing only five years after their conquest in 43 AD.

The name Uphill is said to be a corruption of *Hubba's Pill*, or Creek, or alternatively the settlement above the Pylle – apparently not a reference to the nearby hill but to the creek off the River Axe. *Hubba*, a Danish chieftain who raided these shores, was slain with 800 of his men when he landed at Combwich on the River Parrett in 878 AD with a fleet of war galleys. The Domesday Book, the statistical survey of England completed in 1086 by William I (Conqueror) and compiled most certainly for taxation purposes, records Uphill as *Opopille*.

From the 17th century cattle and sheep were imported from South Wales and later, salt, fish, coal, slate and timber. Exports included lead, zinc, iron and limestone and also bricks and tiles from the former nearby brickworks. The harbour closed in the mid-1940's and now is just an anchorage for pleasure craft.

When sea bathing and the habit of sea-water drinking became medically fashionable in England in the 17th and 18th centuries, it was to re-introduce the idea from the Romans.

This was believed to be a cure for all manner of ailments and the leisure activities of swimming and promenading did not become popular until well into the 1800's, particularly in the River Severn estuary with the disadvantage of its muddy waters and exposed mud flats at low tide. The earliest recorded venture to publicise seaside resorting in the Bristol Channel region was in 1797 at Uphill. This, however, was not successful and it was at nearby Weston-super-Mare that development started and the first hotel was built about 1810 and which after much expansion is now known as the Royal Hotel. Since then Weston-super-Mare has rapidly grown whilst Uphill remains a quiet and contented neighbour.

At the junction of the A370 from Weston-super-Mare with Uphill Road South is Uphill Manor or The Castle. Built in the early 19th century by Rev. Jonathan Gregg, by 1828 it had been considerably enlarged and the tower and mock castellated work added. Along Uphill Road South, on the right, is St. Nicholas Church, a Victorian building of 1844. Soon after, on the left and opposite the chapel, is the oldest building in Uphill, Rose Cottage, which dates from Tudor times of c1545. In 1793 Hannah More, who dedicated herself to helping the poor people of Mendip, came to stay here just for the sea-bathing, then still in its infancy.

Turning into Uphill Way on the right, with Uphill Court on the corner, pass the Ship Inn (c.1830) and then note Ynishir Terrace, also on the right. These houses were built in 1911 by Col. C.E. Whitting of Uphill Grange, formerly of Ynishir in South Wales and owner of coal mines in that area. Number 72 was used as a police station from 1911 until 1939. The Dolphin (18th century) is the older of the two local inns. Across the road on the corner of Old Church Road is the Old Hall, once used as the village meeting hall. Formerly called Crook's House it was built in the early 1700's. It is now a restaurant and tea rooms.

Almost opposite and at the foot of the hill is an area for parking – a convenient point to leave a car for the start of the

West Mendip Way.

Uphill has adequate overnight accommodation of most descriptions and there is a post office and general stores in the village. There are public toilets near the corner with Links Road and it is at this corner that the West Mendip Way begins.

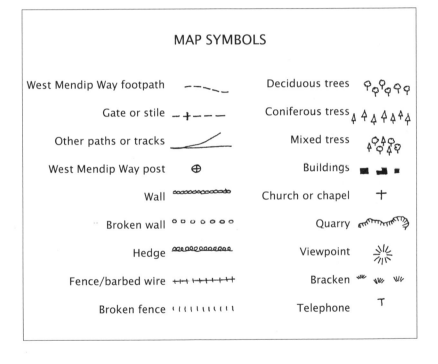

MAP SYMBOLS

West Mendip Way footpath	— — — _ _	Deciduous trees	
Gate or stile	_ + _ _ _	Coniferous tress	
Other paths or tracks		Mixed tress	
West Mendip Way post	⊕	Buildings	
Wall		Church or chapel	+
Broken wall	○ ○ ○ ○ ○ ○ ○	Quarry	
Hedge		Viewpoint	
Fence/barbed wire	+++ +++++++	Bracken	
Broken fence	(((((((((	Telephone	T

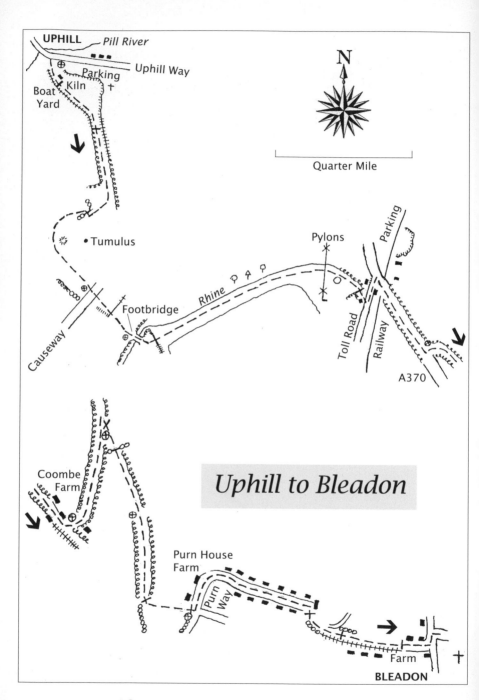

UPHILL — Pill River

Parking

Uphill Way

Kiln

Boat Yard

N

Quarter Mile

Tumulus

Pylons

Parking

Rhine

Footbridge

Causeway

Toll Road

Railway

A370

Coombe Farm

Uphill to Bleadon

Purn House Farm

Purn Way

Farm

BLEADON

1 Uphill to Bleadon

Distance:	3.25 miles (5.2 kms)
Maps:	Opposite and OS Explorer 153
Map Reference:	314585
Going:	It is a level walk to Coombe Farm, other than for the hillock with the tumulus, and after the partial ascent of Purn Hill it is downhill and then level to the village.

At the sea defence wall and floodgate there is a commemorative plaque that indicates the start of the West Mendip Way, opened on 24th May, 1979.

Walk straight ahead and follow the track through the boat centre.

On the right is the slipway and the yard with its varied display of craft alongside the pill, or creek. Quarrying operations here in 1826, on the left, resulted in the discovery of the first cave and two more caves were uncovered at a later date revealing bones of man and many extinct animals. The finds are now exhibited in the Woodspring Museum in Weston-super-Mare. There was also the discovery of 129 silver and copper coins in a fissure but this and the other caves have now been quarried away. The lowest cave, clearly visible with the largest entrance about six feet above the quarry floor, is thought to be an undisturbed section of the original Uphill Cavern. The quarry is believed to have closed down in the 1920's with one reason being given that further work would disrupt the foundations of the old church on the hill above.

St. Nicholas Church, Windmill site and Quarry at Uphill.

Looking back at the Old Church and Quarry, Uphill.

Pass through the Uphill Nature Reserve and on reaching the field bear to the right and away from the track to ascend and follow the lower contours, to the right, around Walborough Hill.

This is capped by the tumulus on the left. On looking back, the Norman church of St. Nicholas – perhaps as early as 1080 – is now seen clearly, sitting proudly on its rocky promontory. The most logical reason for this siting is that centuries ago, when the flat land of central Somerset was permanently of a marshy nature, or even entirely under water, the obvious place to build any fortification or sanctuary was on high ground.

Even the earliest of dwellings or burial chambers are known to have been built on hills as protection against invaders or development.

There are two legends attached to the building of this church. The first is that the villagers started to build at the base of the hill but St. Nicholas (patron saint of virgins, boys, sailors and the worshipful company of parish clerks to the city of London) disagreed. When the work was restarted by day at the base then the stone and building materials would be moved each night to the summit. It was eventually realised that the unequalled power of St. Nicholas was so great that his wishes should be obeyed and so the church was completed in the position that it still commands.

The other story told is that two sea-faring men of the village contributed much finance to the building of the church and the nautical fraternity agreed with them that it should be sited where all mariners could use it as a navigational aid. The father and son who were responsible for this financing were themselves shipwrecked and were the first people to be buried in the churchyard.

Two interesting graves, found near the west wall, are of: Major George P. Ewens, the first editor of the Salvation Army magazine *War Cry*, who lived in nearby New Church Road for a number of years prior to his death in 1926; and Frank Castle Froest, a former CID superintendent of Scotland Yard who authorised Detective Chief Inspector Walter Devy to arrest the murderer Dr. Crippen in July, 1910, on board the liner *Montrose*. This was made possible by the very first transatlantic ship's wireless message. On his retirement from the police force Superintendent Froest became Hon. Superintendent of the Royal West of England Sanatorium, more recently known as the Royal Hospital (now residential homes) near the golf course between Weston-super-Mare and Uphill. He died in 1930.

After the building of the new church it was decided that no more baptisms were to be held in the old one so, in 1891, the Norman font was transferred to ensure its safety and continued use. The Victorian font was not made redundant, however, but was cut vertically into two equal parts, transported up the hill to the old church, and is now positioned to form supports for the altar – a most unusual function. On the tower is another oddity: a three-headed gargoyle, said to be the only one of its kind in Europe. The nave of the church has been roofless since 1864 but the tower and chancel are still covered.

A little to the east of the church is the site of Uphill Windmill. Formerly it was a traditional hilltop beacon site to warn of invaders such as the Vikings in the 9th century or the Spanish Armada in the 16th. In the 13th century there was a windmill, but, it is believed, during the time of King Henry VIII and the Spanish Armada, it was converted into a watch-tower and artillery post. Corn was once grown on the slopes of this hill and another windmill was built in the late 18th century but became derelict by 1829. It was also used as a look-out tower in the Napoleonic Wars during the early 19th century and again during the First World War. It was rebuilt and castellated in 1934 for use as an observatory and during the Second World War it was used by the Royal Observer Corps.

In spring the hillside is covered with the yellow flowers of the kidney vetch, horseshoe vetch, birdsfoot–trefoil, yellow ruttle and cowslips. In the summer will follow various types of orchids, hawkweeds, wild thyme, yellow rockrose, lady's bedstraw and agrimony. Thistles that can be found are the musk, stemless and carline. The wide variety of plants here provide a haven for the caterpillars of the blue, small copper and marbled white butterflies. The rare Somerset grass (*koeleria vallesiana*) was first recorded here in 1726 and also very rare is the honewart (*trinia glauca*).

Brean Down, the 1.5 miles (2.4 kms) long headland in the west rising to 320 feet (97.5 metres) above sea level with splendid cliffs on either side, is National Trust property and a bird sanctuary and nature reserve. Many species of gulls, sea ducks and freshwater ducks can be identified in this area which includes the kittiwake, named after its courtship cries of 'kitt-ee-wayke', the eider, which is the largest and most robust of the sea ducks and the mallard, which is the most numerous and widespread of our ducks. Rare sightings have also been made of the great and Arctic skuas, marsh harrier and peregrine. The steep, south-facing rocky slopes of Brean Down are also the main British location for the white rockrose (*helianthemum appenninum*). In early summer the white flowers are quite conspicuous and it also grows on Purn Hill. It is only found elsewhere in Britain near Torbay in Devon.

There is evidence that this was once a prehistoric occupation site, including tumuli, and an Iron Age settlement was built here and later a mid- 4th century Roman temple. At the tip of the headland is the remains of a fort built in 1867 against threatened invasion from the French and the Second World War in 1939 brought more installations. An historic occasion on 18th May, 1897 was recorded when Marconi was experimenting in the very early days of wireless telegraphy. The signals he transmitted from Lavernock, near Penarth in South Wales, nine miles (14.5 kms) away to the north-west across the Bristol Channel, were received here.

To the right of Brean Down is Black Rock in the Axe estuary and then beyond is Weston-super-Mare overlooked by Worlebury Hill.

The confluence of the Pill and the Axe becomes evident close by so continue around Walborough Hill and where a causeway is seen alongside the Axe, cross and continue ahead to the stile.

The variety of birds identifiable in this area is both numerous and exciting. Many sea birds, wildfowl or wading birds are present, and spring or autumn would be the best times to see all categories of residents, visitors and passing migrants. The

21

oyster catcher, with its black and white plumage and long orange bill, is the most conspicuous of the wading birds that inhabit our shores, and the curlew is Britain's largest wader, recognised by the grey-brown plumage, long legs and downward-curved bill. The snipe, often seen further inland, has brown-streaked and patterned plumage, a boldly striped head and a long straight bill. Its flight is zigzag and a quavering humming can be heard which is produced as the outer tail feathers vibrate in the wind.

> *Go straight ahead almost in a south-east direction to the footbridge and cross the rhine, or ditch. Pass through the gate a few steps away, ahead and towards the left, and then keep straight on between the two rhines.*

The Grange becomes visible between the trees, in a northerly direction, to the left. This was built by Thomas Gregg in the mid-18th century and it was his father, the Rev. Jonathan Gregg, who built Uphill Castle.

> *On reaching Toll Road, turn left.*

To the right is the former Bleadon and Uphill Halt where no trains have stopped since the 1960's. The original toll road, owned by the Grange, curved at this point and can be seen incorporated into the garden of West View opposite as it then straightened to cross the railway at right angles. Toll Gate, on the left, is the former toll-house, believed to have been built in the early 19th century, but since enlarged and modernised and it was as long ago as 1908 that a toll was last paid. The windmill, erected in about 1965, was an unsuccessful attempt to generate enough power to provide the house with electric lighting as gas was still in use until about 1966.

> *Turn right to follow the main road (A370) and cross the railway.*

This road was widened and straightened in 1934 with this new bridge being built over the railway and it was then that the toll road became unused for through traffic. Looking to the left from the bridge is an overgrown rock face of a former quarry. When the Bristol and Exeter railway was cut through here in 1841, stone from here was used as ballast for the track. It is thought that soon after the railway was built the quarry closed down.

Under the direction of Isambard Kingdom Brunel, who also designed and built the S.S. *Great Britain* and the Clifton Suspension Bridge in Bristol, the railway navvies became quarrelsome with him concerning their wages. An ugly scene was about to develop so a messenger was sent to inform Mr. Knyfton of Uphill Castle, who was a magistrate. On arrival he was shouted and sworn at and shown much contempt by the raised pick-axes and shovels that confronted him. On reading the Riot Act and the threat of cavalry troops being sent from Horfield Barracks in Bristol to quell the disturbance Mr Knyfton silenced the angry mob and work continued.

The road bridge a little further along the railway to the left is Devil's Bridge (named after Squire Payne of Uphill Grange, often referred to as 'that old devil'). It is reputed to be the highest single-span brick bridge in Somerset. Squire Payne, who owned all the land around, was compelled by an act of parliament to sell some of it for this railway and he stipulated that a station should be built for his own private use. This was completed and was located next to Toll Road, to the right of the main road, but as he drove such a hard bargain and no mention of trains was included in the agreement no trains ever stopped there in his lifetime.

Turn left at the lane and left again just after Coombe Farm, along the track.

It is said that if one ascends this rough track at midnight on the anniversary of the battle of Sedgemoor the voices of men can be heard singing and shouting on their return from that ill-fated rebellion of 6th July 1685.

Before the housing estate pass through the gate on the right.

Purn Hill is ahead, believed to be the site of a Celtic camp and a view of Bleadon appears in the south-east. Beyond the large circular slurry tank (350,000 gallons/1,591,100 litres) is the rear of the white buildings of the 17th century manor house. Beyond, the disused South Hill quarry is also seen and this ceased extracting stone in 1959. To the left in the north-east on the slopes of Bleadon Hill a Celtic field system is said to have been worked.

Cross the field towards Bleadon and afterwards a well-defined path continues with the hawthorn hedge on the left. Keep ahead on the main path (ignore the stile on the left that was the original route and still marked on the latest O/S maps), pass over the stile and cross the field to the gate. At the road turn left along Purn Way.

Purn House Farm is on the left. The farmhouse was designed by Robert Adams, the Scottish architect in the latter half of the 18th century. He was responsible for some very fine works in the neo-classical style, particularly with the planning and decoration of the interiors. His achievements include Harewood House, Osterley Park, Syon House, Luton Hoo, Kenwood House and Kedleston Hall.

Bear right with the bend in the lane and keep straight ahead along the road between the houses. At the pink Westdown Cottage turn right through the gate and along the tarmac drive. As the drive turns left, keep ahead with the view of the church. Keep the fence and houses on the right and pass through the gate at Whitegate Farm.

The new houses on the right are built on an Iron Age burial site of c100 BC. In 1997 six circular pits were discovered, two of which contained the skeletons of a man and a woman, both buried in a crouched position. Other pits contained animal bones, fragments of pottery and an iron brooch.

Continue along Rectory Lane to the main road in Bleadon.

Several definitions are given for the name of this village but the earliest would probably be the Celtic *Blai,* meaning a wolf, and *Don*, a hill. Another interpretation is from *Bleodun* or the blue-coloured down, mottled green and grey where limestone occurs.

The well-known local tale is that when the Danes came plundering inland the villagers fled to the hills, except for a lame woman who hid. As the invaders pursued the inhabitants this woman bravely crept to where the enemy ships were tied (said to be at the River Axe) and cast them adrift. Seeing the Danes retreat cut off, the locals seized the advantage and a terrible massacre took place. Since then the site of the battle has been known as *Bleed Down*. The Normans state it as *Bledone* in the Domesday Book.

The chancel is the oldest section of the church dedicated to St.Peter and St.Paul, and dates from 1317. One of only about 60 remaining in Britain, of which 20 are in Somerset, the mediaeval octagonal stone pulpit, richly carved with Tudor flowers and vines, was erected in c.1460. The tub-shaped font is thought to be Norman but the pedestal and steps are later additions. The little stone angel by the two arches in the north wall is possibly Saxon but the lower head is either 13th or 14th century. The tiles in the north wall arch are also of a similar date and were dug from the churchyard and it is possible that they formed the flooring of the original chancel. The plastered wagon roof is the rounded universal type used in the West Country.

The lofty tower was built in the early 15th century and is

Right: Bleadon Parish Church and the Cross.

Below: The interior of St. Peter and St. Paul's Church, Bleadon.

Right: The stone pulpit in Bleadon Church dating from c1460.

typical of the West Mendip design known as the triple-windowed perpendicular style. Five of the six bells were cast at the foundry of the Bilbie family of Chew Stoke in 1711 and the sixth by Taylors of Loughborough in 1925. There are some interesting gargoyles, some rather quaint and now very worn, including a little fellow sitting cross-legged and playing a type of bagpipes. On the south wall of the church, low down on the buttress, is an old mass or scratch dial which often had one line more clearly marked than the others, usually nine a.m. to indicate the normal hour of mass. These scratch dials date to between 12th–15th century. To the left of the south porch is a monument to Aeneas Ranald W. McDonell who was 'Chief of Glengarry' in the Scottish highlands and who died in 1901.

The 14th century cross is badly weathered and has been used as a tethering post for horses but the head was made in the 19th century. Close by on the wall of Church Cottages is a date of 1869 and the initials E.P. These commemorate the building of a bicycle here by Ernest Parker, a blacksmith. Well Cottage, near the post office, has two pumps – a reminder of the old days when almost every house in the lower part of Bleadon had a well.

Accommodation is very limited in the village but camping and caravanning facilities are to be found within the parish. There is short-term parking near the village hall and public toilets are adjacent. A post office and general stores is also located near the church.

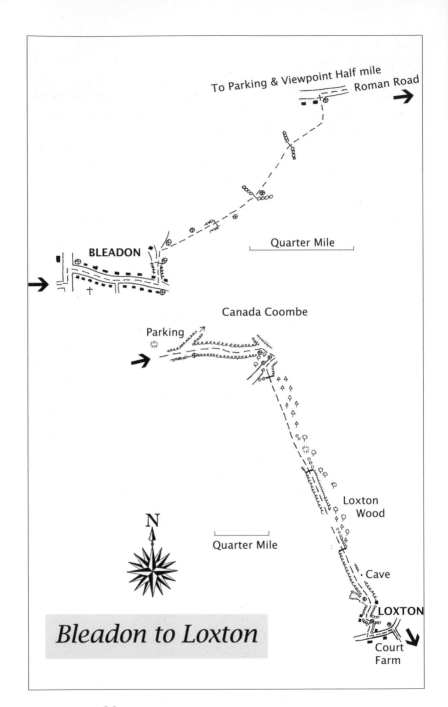

To Parking & Viewpoint Half mile

Roman Road

Quarter Mile

BLEADON

Canada Coombe

Parking

Loxton
Wood

Cave

N

Quarter Mile

LOXTON

Court
Farm

Bleadon to Loxton

2 Bleadon to Loxton

Distance:	3.5 miles (5.6 kms)
Maps:	Opposite & OS Explorer 153
Map Reference:	341570
Going:	After the climb of Hellenge Hill to Bleadon Hill the route levels along Roman Road before the ascent of Loxton Hill and then downhill to Loxton.

Turn left at the main road and then right along Shiplate Road. (Be very cautious at this dangerous corner.)

On the right is Old School Lane and on the corner is the old school, built in 1854 and closed in 1964. Just beyond Birch Avenue are a couple of stone plaques set into the wall. The memorial plaque is 'In Memory of the Fallen 1914-1918.' This was once incorporated in the wall of the former Methodist School Room, built on this site in 1920 and demolished in 1967.

After approximately 200 yards (less than 200 metres) from Birch Avenue and just after the start of the sloping grass verge turn left up the lane, alongside 'Beechfield'. Just before the private drive bear right through the gate and into the field. Take the right-hand path diagonally up Hellenge Hill (owned by Avon Wildlife Trust), heading north-east to the stile. Bear only a little to the left, still north-east, and pass a small directional post about 100 yards (almost 100 metres) from the stile. Still ascending slightly continue to the stone stile.

Looking along the coast from Brean Down, in the west, can be seen the villages of Brean and then Berrow, in the south-west. The town of Burnham-on-Sea is in the south-south-west and the lighthouse is visible and which was built in 1834 and lit by oil up to 1970. Although rising in Dorset the River Parrett is Somerset's longest, at 36 miles (58 kms), and the mouth can be clearly seen in fine weather. The Bridgwater Bay Nature Reserve includes the Parrett Estuary and also Steart Island, basically shingle, mud and sand, but this muddy and bleak stretch of coast is a wintering area for many species of wild-fowl and waders. It is also a rich fishing ground for shrimps, eels and flounders which are caught by fishermen using 'mud horses' to slide across the mud to reach their nets at low tide. Beyond is visible the nuclear power station of Hinkley Point (to the right of Burnham-on-Sea and in the south-west) and the coastal views extend to Foreland Point in Devon. This coast has one of the highest tides in the world and the normal rise and fall in the Bristol Channel has a range of 35 feet (10.7 metres). Since the 17th century the deserted beaches of Somerset have been popular with smugglers, and the county's ship owners and sea captains were involved in the lucrative trades of wine and slavery.

The River Axe, which meanders its way nearby towards the coast, identifies the boundary once ruled by the Celts and it is believed that they might have given the river the name of *Esk*, *Usk* or *Es*, meaning water.

Brent Knoll, in the south, that 457 feet (139 metres) high noble hill rising from the Somerset Levels, once known as the Isle of Frogs, was probably used as a beacon, particularly to warn of Danish invasion. The Iron Age fort on the summit provided shelter for the Saxons when the Danes invaded and it is on the south side at Battleborough where the Saxon King Alfred and the Danes clashed. Brent Knoll was an island when these lowlands were permanently flooded but the land has now been well drained and sea defences built and so boats will never again ferry passengers or cargo between the hills.

30

The land stretching from the coast to Glastonbury Tor in the distant south-east, geographically the Valley of the River Brue, was once known as Brent Marsh. However, the legend of King Arthur of Camelot and his knights has become so romantically linked with Glastonbury and the hill fort at South Cadbury that this land is now known as the Vale of Avalon. Once an area of shallow lakes and stagnant marshes, and occasionally flooded by the sea, it was inhabited by the Celts who built lakeside villages with houses raised on poles or stilts. Many objects have been recovered, including a 16 feet (4.9 metres) dug-out canoe. These villages flourished from about 250 BC until just after the Roman invasion.

Arriving from mainland Europe it is believed that the Celts first settled in the British Isles about 700 BC bringing the art of iron smelting and introducing the Iron Age. Although established in Wales, Scotland and Ireland, many of the Celts were attacked and forced to flee to Wales and the West Country by the Romans and later, in the 5th century, by the Saxons and other Germanic people that invaded the country. Many of the hill forts and settlements that were built during their occupation still survive, such as Brent Knoll, as well as evidence of their lake and marsh villages.

Peat cutting has revealed even earlier traces of civilisation – Neolithic trackways laid with hazel and birch twigs and branches. Nearly 40 different trackways have been found on the Somerset Levels, the oldest being the Sweet Track, built about 3,200 BC, possibly the oldest roadway in the world. Peat, decomposed vegetation of at least 5,000 years old, was once used for fuel around here but is now cut in vast quantities for gardeners and horticulturists.

The monastic community of Glastonbury cut the first main artificial waterway, the Mark Yeo, about 1700 to reclaim land and link the Axe and Brue rivers. The monks also diverted streams to develop the rivers for transport to areas of their estates such as at Pilton where they planted vines as early as the 13th century. It was between 1790 and 1810 that the major

31

land reclamation schemes were started, by acts of parliament, and the main watercourses, ditches, or rhines, cut.

Whilst this drainage is advantageous to dairy farmers, giving them some of the richest grazing land in the country, the total drainage of this area would spell disaster and extinction for many forms of wildlife. At present this wet and soggy environment is ideal for some threatened and endangered species of insect, bird and plant life, and it is the finest breeding ground in the south-west for wading birds.

Beyond this level landscape is the low, narrow range of the Polden Hills. The battle of Sedgemoor in 1685, the last battle fought on English soil, took place just over these hills on the outskirts of Westonzoyland. The son of King Charles II, James, the Duke of Monmouth, rallied an army, comprised mainly of farmers, cloth-workers, miners and the like, armed with pitchforks, spades and axes, to seize the throne of England – the Pitchfork Rebellion. Monmouth's rebel army became cornered and there followed a terrible massacre in which Monmouth suffered a disastrous defeat. The wounded and scattered rebels were rounded up, imprisoned in the Parish Church of St. Mary, and many of those that did not die of their injuries were hanged and buried at the battleground. The Duke was captured and executed at the Tower of London. Lord Chief Justice Jeffreys was authorised by James II to punish the rebels and his widespread 'Bloody Assizes' became feared by all.

From the stone stile cross the field, slightly diagonally left and still north-east, to the wooden stile. Bear left and up to the right of the last house to the stile and road.

Roman Road was once known as Golf Course Road as there was an 18-hole course behind the houses across the road and on the left. It was taken over by the army in 1939 and barrage balloons and anti-aircraft guns were erected, but the green keeper's cottage still stands as a memorial to this pre-war era. There are camping and caravanning possibilities in this immediate vicinity.

Turn right on the road.

Although opinions are divided, this road is thought to have been the direct link between Charterhouse and Uphill when the Romans transported lead from the central Mendip area.

When the brow of Bleadon Hill is reached, at 450 feet (137 metres) there are panoramic views of the South Wales coast. The resort of Barry Island can be seen in the west-north-west and just to the right is Wenvoe television transmitter. The islands of Steep Holm and Flat Holm are in the centre of the busy shipping lanes of the Bristol Channel. Steep Holm, a bird sanctuary controlled by the Kenneth Allsop Trust, is uninhabited. In 1867 it was fortified and garrisoned and was again occupied by troops in 1939. The Vikings occupied both islands in the 9th century and Danish pirates later took refuge on Steep Holm in 918 AD. The name *Holm* is Scandinavian, meaning an island either in a lake or river, and given to these islands by the Norsemen.

On a clear day vision is extended to almost 50 miles (80 kms) a few degrees to the right of north-west to the 2,906 feet (886 metres) summit of Pen-y-Fan in the Brecon Beacons. Newport docks alongside the channel can be seen further to the right.

Worlebury Hill camp, away to the north-west overlooking Weston-super-Mare (probably at one time the best defended hill fort in the area), was built and inhabited in the Iron Age by the Celts since c300 BC. It has been conjectured that when the Romans arrived this fort was invaded and the occupiers slaughtered as about 20 skeletons have been found and many had terrible wounds.

Before 1800 Weston-super-Mare, now the largest resort on the Bristol Channel, was a small fishing village, but when sea-bathing became popular it became successful mainly because of the wide spacious sands and bracing sea breezes.

Along the coast to the right at north-north-east is Clevedon with its strong literary associations. Samuel Taylor Coleridge began his married life there in 1795. Alfred Tennyson wrote there one of his finest works, 'In Memoriam', which reflected his grief at the loss of his dear friend Arthur Hallam, the British essayist, buried in the parish churchyard. The novelist William Thackeray often visited Clevedon Court (c1320) where he wrote most of his *Vanity Fair.*

Where the road bends to the left continue ahead along the bridlepath, still following the course of the Roman road. Turn right on the rough and stony track that ascends to another, turn to the right and then bear to the left. Follow the track alongside the plantation until the brow of Loxton Hill is reached at about 527 feet (161 metres).

Below, to the left, is the tiny village of Christon. The church of St. Mary has some splendid yew trees in the churchyard, and some herringbone masonry on the outside of the north wall of the chancel is of the earliest work and has been dated to c1080. Christon also has a gazebo, and two smaller objects of interest are the Victorian letterbox, still in use, and the cast-iron pump with a stone trough, now disused.

When the M5 motorway was being built through the Lox Yeo Valley nearby an Iron Age settlement was uncovered. The site, on the knoll just above the valley floor, was the only example of its type on Mendip as usually a camp was built much higher. Evidence of a round timber building came to light, and 13 skeletons were found, one wearing an iron bracelet.

Across the motorway and nestling at the foot of Barton Hill, to the north of Wavering Down, is the Hamlet of Barton. In the hillside above is a cave that is the only known wolf den on Mendip.

Beyond Barton in the east is St. James, the parish church of

Above: Crook Peak and Wavering Down from Loxton Hill.

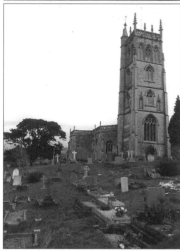

Left: St. James Church, Winscombe, and the 600 year-old yew tree.

Right: Loxton Hunting Lodge with North Lodge on the right.

Winscombe. This is the only point of the West Mendip Way from which it is visible and the tower is of the triple-windowed perpendicular type and one of the finest examples of the sixty remaining in Somerset. The enormous yew in the churchyard has a girth of nearly 20 feet (6.1 metres) and is said to be at least 600 years old. This splendid church was originally Norman but the only survivors from this period are the font and the piscina on the south wall of the chancel. Under the wooden lid of the bowl of the font are marks that show where the cover was once locked by staples or clasps. In 1236 it was decreed that all fonts were to be locked as a precaution against the holy water being used for the purpose of sorcery.

Further to the right is Crook Peak. Not the highest but the most conspicuous peak on the Mendip Hills, this was an ideal vantage point on which to light warning beacon fires.

Loxton Wood comprises a mixed tree species including larch, spruce, ash and beech, but is mainly coniferous. Some ash was used from here during the second World War to build parts for the Mosquito bomber, the most successful and versatile military aircraft of its time. As imported supplies of other top quality wood diminished so ash was used by some of the local villagers who helped with the lightweight wooden construction of the fuselage and wings in their own homes and gardens.

Green woodpeckers — the largest of the species — are quite numerous in this locality, and can be recognised by the laughing cry during its undulating flight, and by the crimson crown, bright green plumage with paler green underparts and a yellow rump. Many pheasants and partridges are also often seen as they are bred nearby.

Further down the hill and close to the track on the left is Loxton Cave, hidden from view along an overgrown path and at the base of a vertical rock face. Once there were plans to open this well-decorated cavern to the public but nothing materialised. As you reach Hillview Road, on the right is the disused Loxton Quarry where three small caves were revealed.

Above left: Victorian lamp-post and letter box in Loxton.

Above right: Loxton churchyard Cross.

Right: The squint, or hagioscope, in the porch of St. Andrew's Church, Loxton.

> *Follow the road down to the entrance of the Hunting Lodge.*

Built in 1873, this was used as a summer retreat by Henry Tiarks for fox hunting. The North Lodge on the right was added in 1939.

> *At the old pump on the corner the footpath turns and descends to the right.*

This pump was erected in about 1884 and was last used in the 1930's. The old school, built in about 1878, was last used for education in about 1961.

Just before the road is a seat perfectly situated below the high walls of the Hunting Lodge in a peaceful and sheltered position. The former chapel on the left was built in about 1884 but was given to the villagers in 1937 for use as a village hall. At the roadside, just to the right, are a Victorian letterbox and a restored iron lamp-post commemorating 60 years of Queen Victoria's reign. Opposite is the Old Rectory; the east wing was built in 1873, the rest added in about 1884. There are magnificent Lebanon cedar and cypress in the rear garden.

> *Turn left at the road.*

The hidden and easily missed church of St. Andrew was probably built on Saxon foundations. There are traces of Norman and early English architecture in the tower. Inside the porch is a squint, or hagioscope – a square hole cut through the wall and barred with an iron grating. Perhaps it enabled lepers, who were not allowed to mix with the congregation, to watch the service, but the usual explanation is that an attendant could judge the precise moment during a service when the sanctus bell should be rung. The stained glass dates from the 14th century as most probably does the font. One of the few remaining, the beautiful 15th century stone pulpit was cut from a single block of stone. Part of the carved oak screen across the chancel is early 16th century but otherwise much of the original interior has been moved, renovated or replaced. In the vestry is a complete list of rectors since William de Botesford in 1298. The 15th century churchyard cross by the old yew tree had its upper section restored in 1910.

Spelt *Lochestone* in the Domesday Book, it has been suggested that the first syllable in Loxton could be from the Norse word *lax*, meaning salmon, but it is perhaps more likely that the name in this case came from a former Saxon landowner. Accommodation is probably not available, there being not even a public house, and car parking is very restricted. A garage workshop and a post office are to be found by turning to the right on reaching the road from the Hunting Lodge. This short diversion will re-join the West Mendip Way just before crossing the motorway but will miss the delightful setting of St. Andrew's Church.

The village of Loxton with Loxton Hill at the top right.

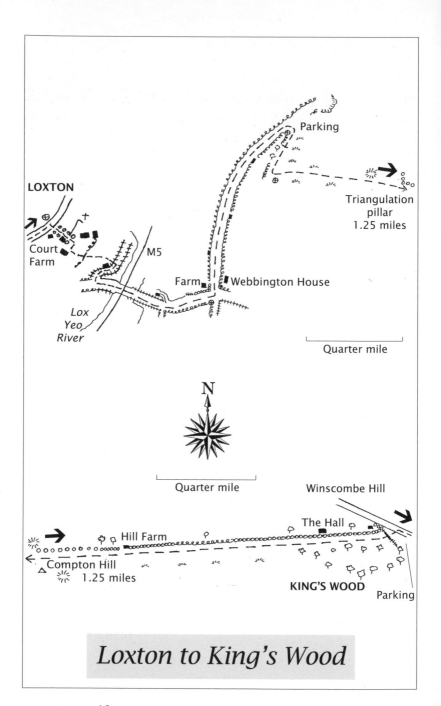

LOXTON

Court Farm

M5

Parking

Triangulation pillar
1.25 miles

Farm Webbington House

Lox
Yeo
River

Quarter mile

N

Quarter mile

Winscombe Hill

The Hall

Hill Farm

Compton Hill
1.25 miles

KING'S WOOD

Parking

Loxton to King's Wood

3 Loxton to King's Wood

Distance:	3.5 miles (5.6 kms)
Maps:	Opposite & OS Explorer 153
Map Reference:	375558
Going:	Generally an uphill walk to Wavering Down and then a descent to King's Wood with the first mile (1.6 kms) of road walking and the rest a bridleway.

Court Farm is believed to be a 13th century farmhouse but has a date of c1530 on the wall and was used at one time as a courthouse. A second Victorian lamp-post is situated here by the entrance to the farmhouse.

> *Turn right into Church Lane and at the farmyard turn right over the stile and left through the gate. Head south-east across the field to the little building, follow the track to the right and then turn left to cross over the motorway which has disturbed the peace of this beautiful valley since 1972.*

The Lox Yeo river is formed by the united brooks of Winscombe and Shipham and flows into the river Axe. As Lox may be derived from *lax*, a salmon, and Yeo from the Anglo-Saxon *Ea*, meaning water, this could be translated as salmon river. Salmon did swim up prior to 1802, but the Bleadon floodgates were installed and prevented this and further navigation of all these little rivers.

On the left is 'Forgotten World', a horse-drawn carriage restoration works, wheelwrights and Romany museum. Open from May to October it also supports a café that could provide

Webbington Hotel at the foot of Crook Peak.

Rock outcrop on the summit of Crook Peak.

a welcome 'cuppa' for the thirsty traveller. This was the site of a former dairy in the early 1900's and a sheepwash nearby was used by farmers up to the 1950's. Ahead and below Crook Peak is the half-timbered Edwardian building of Webbington House. Once the centre of fox hunting it has become known in recent years as a hotel, country club and conference centre.

Henry Tiarks of Loxton Hunting Lodge had Webbington House built as a wedding present for his son Herman in about 1901. It was designed by Sir Edward Lutyens but the appearance is spoilt by later additions. Prior to it being built Herman lived at Webbington Farm on the corner of Barton Road. It has been said that a ghost was seen at the bottom of the staircase in the farmhouse and that when Herman married and moved to his new house the ghost followed him. Fearing that stories of this apparition would frighten the servants away the sightings were not spoken of.

Originally popular with 18th century squires, fox-hunting on Mendip was established mainly by the determination of Herman Tiarks and his brother Frank. There was much opposition to this sport even then, but the Mendip hunt was founded in 1914, only to cease again soon after because of the outbreak of war. It was revived in 1920, and in 1922 the pack was known as the Mendip following the kennels being moved to Priddy. Foxhounds are again kennelled at Webbington, and are now known as the Weston and Banwell harriers.

Turn left along Barton Road passing The Lodge, built for and at the same time as Webbington House, and situated at the original entrance. Turn right after The Paddock, where a grassy area just before a disused quarry may be suitable for car parking.

Crook Peak, above, is taken from the ancient British word *Cruc*, meaning a peak or pointed hill. This commanding position made an ideal vantage point to light beacon-fires in times of danger, and war, and to warn of impending invasion.

Follow the bridleway to the right and then keep straight ahead to pass behind The Paddock and then bear left to begin a long hard climb that passes below the rocky summit of Crook Peak high up on the right. The path traverses the gorse-covered hillside away from and above the sheer face of the old quarry, and when two routes become evident either one will lead to a broad grass track.

The views are now becoming quite magnificent but because of the nature of the landscape not all landmarks are going to be seen from any one position. Christon is quite close in the north-west just across the valley and, with binoculars, even the Victorian letterbox and the iron pump by the wall of Christon Court can be identified. Slightly to the right but at twice the distance is the water tower of RAF Locking.

Beyond that, north-north-west at about 7.5 miles (12 kms) is St. Thomas's Head by Woodspring Bay. Nearby is Woodspring Priory that is believed to have been founded in 1210, being converted from a chapel in the Manor of Worspring and dedicated to St. Thomas, the Martyr of Canterbury. Thomas a Becket, Archbishop of Canterbury, was murdered in the cathedral in 1170 by four knights, one of whom was Reginald Fitzurse, owner of Worspring Manor. At the time of the murder blood was collected in wooden cups and many years later one was taken to the priory to be treasured by the monks. During the time of the Reformation and Dissolution of the Monasteries (1536-1539, when Henry VIII confiscated church property) the monks transferred the precious cup to Kewstoke Church. During repairs in this church in 1849 a small wooden cup was discovered behind carved stone-work. The cup contained samples of a dry dark substance that was identified as blood. This vessel is now in the care of Taunton museum.

The tower on Banwell Hill, in the north, was built by Bishop Law in about 1840; he also planted the avenue of trees and laid out the paths. The building to the right is a Bristol Waterworks water treatment plant. In the north-east is Sandford Hill, now permanently scarred by quarrying operations.

On reaching the broad track bear left away from Crook Peak.

Close by, on the right and to the south of Compton Hill, is Compton Bishop, the settlement in a hollow or combe of the hills, once known as Compton Episcopi.

The church of St. Andrew was consecrated in 1236 by Bishop Jocelin. The oldest object inside is the Norman font with the beautiful cone-shaped oak cover being inscribed with the later date of 1617. This font also has evidence of clasps once used to protect the holy water. The 14th century carved stone pulpit is again one of the best examples in Somerset, but the fifth panel was added in 1852. In the floor are some tombstones dating from 1690-1720, and in the churchyard stands the 14th century headless cross, probably the only memorial to the dead before individual gravestones were used.

Beyond the church is the ridge running south-east from Crook Peak in which there are five caves. One, Denny's Hole, is named after St. Dennis, and there once was a chapel dedicated to him in the village. This cave was used during the Second World War by the Home Guard.

Just over this ridge at Rackley, on the banks of the Cheddar Yeo River, was once a most important wharf said to have been used by the Romans to transport lead ingots from their mines to Uphill. Before the Drainage Act of 1802 this river was navigable as far as Hythe, another important port near Cheddar. Salt, slate, coal and timber were unloaded and stone, lead and iron exported. The river is clearly seen in the south-east with Nyland Hill beyond; Cheddar Reservoir and the village are towards the left.

After a slight descent the route continues uphill.

Banwell Castle in the north, to the left, can now be seen more clearly. It is not of mediaeval construction, despite its appearance, but was built in about 1845 for Joseph Dyer Sympson and is still in private ownership. A plaque above the northern gateway bears the following proclamation: 'Built in the 19th century, and of no historical interest. Kindly observe that this Englishman's castle is his home, and do not intrude.'

The hill to the right is crowned by a prehistoric camp and between this and Sandford Quarry, but at the further distance of about five miles (8 kms) is the spire of St. Andrew's Church, Congresbury, one of so many visible from these hills. Further to the right, in the north-east at the same distance, is All Saints

45

Looking back to Crook Peak from the path leading to Wavering Down.

Cheddar Reservoir from the triangulation pillar on Wavering Down.

Church tower in Wrington. It is in the churchyard here that Hannah More (1745-1833) is buried.

In the same direction but close by on the Maxmills Meadows is Winscombe. This was at one time one of the many isolated manors belonging to the Church of Glastonbury but is now united with Woodborough, once a small and neighbouring hamlet. To the east of Winscombe and in line with Dolebury Hill are some white buildings of Sidcot School. Formerly a Quaker co-educational establishment founded in 1808 it was built on the site of an earlier boys' school and meeting house of 1699. Dolebury Hill Fort is an excellent example of an Iron Age fortress. It was the largest and one of the most heavily guarded and is now the finest on or around Mendip. A little to the right in the east-north-east is Shipham.

The short turf underfoot is ideal for walking and in fine weather the effort to reach the triangulation pillar on the summit of Wavering Down is truly rewarded by the beauty of the surroundings.

At a height of 690 feet (210 metres) it is 62 feet (19 metres) higher than Crook Peak, and in clear weather there is a magnificent 360-degree panoramic view. Some of the finest views in Somerset are now before you, with the Quantock and Brendon Hills in the south-west, and Somerset's highest hill, Dunkery Beacon on Exmoor at 1,705 feet (520 metres) just to the right in the west-south-west – a dark rounded shape on the distant horizon.

Nearby in the south are the greenhouses of the nurseries at Lower Weare and beyond and to the left in the south-south-east at 5.5 miles (8.8 kms) is Wedmore. The claim to fame there is that at nearby Mudgley Hill King Alfred had a palace. After his great victory over the Danes at Ethandune in 878 AD he entertained his former enemy Guthrum and they both signed a peace treaty. This is commemorated by a small plaque in the south porch of St. Mary's Church and by a sundial on the church wall.

The Mendip Hills and the Somerset Lowlands include hill, moorland, rocky cliffs, wooded valleys, orchard, meadow, marsh and cultivated land. With the coast nearby a wide variety of both resident and migratory birds are present. The patches of gorse and heather provide the skylark with some privacy during the breeding season and you may be serenaded in spring and summer by one of Britain's best-loved birds. The delightful warbling song is usually heard when the bird is in flight, perhaps high in the sky and almost out of sight. As in the case of most male birds it has two objectives; the defence of its territory and to attract females. The English poet, Percy Bysshe Shelley (1792-1822), wrote 'To a Skylark' in 1820 and described it: 'Hail to thee, blithe spirit' and 'As from thy presence showers a rain of melody.' The meadow pipit, another characteristic bird of Mendip, leaves the ground in a fluttering song flight with a tuneless collection of notes as it flies higher but sings more musically as it glides to earth again. This small brown bird is the favourite choice of host to feed the hatched fledglings of the cuckoo. The male cuckoo's monotonous courtship song is, to us, the most eagerly awaited sound in spring, but not so welcomed by the meadow pipit, dunnock, reed warbler, robin, pied wagtail or sedge warbler, whose nests are often chosen by the female cuckoo. She destroys or eats the occupier's eggs then lays her own to be fostered by the host bird who usually offers no resistance.

With the radio mast on Fry's Hill ahead in the east, the West Mendip Way now descends, following a Saxon boundary.

Hill Farm, on the left, is believed to be of Saxon origin. If you reach the shade of King's Wood in the spring or early summer the distinctive aroma of wild garlic will be most noticeable. The much travelled colonising armies of Rome used this herb to ward off infection, in the treatment of coughs and lung diseases, and it also made an effective dressing for wounds.

Many different trees are found, including yew, douglas fir, sycamore, field maple, beech, oak, ash, sweet chestnut and hazel. This wood was one of the first to be included in the Mendip 'forest' which, in the perambulation, or survey, of Mendip in 1298, comprised little more than the manors of Axbridge and Cheddar. Although trees did grow here, chiefly oak, the term 'forest' was generally used to describe the king's land within enclosed boundaries that included wood and moorland and which supported much wildlife. It was used before the Norman Conquest in 1066 and up to mediaeval times, mainly for the hunting of wild boar and red deer. As successive kings gave up more of their own estates to be included so the boundaries of Mendip were revised and extended.

The laurel and rhododendron bushes on the other side of the wall are within the grounds of Winscombe Hall. This was built for the Rev. John Augustus Yatman in 1855 who retired from his Yorkshire curacy to become Squire of Winscombe. The architect was William Railton who also designed Nelson's Column in London and Cardiff Castle. The two end wings were added in 1863 by William Burgess, another fine designer, and the gothic tower was built in 1871. The Hall is now a residential elderly people's home.

Stone Cottage, on the left, was built from a very small quarry that incorporates the rock face in the garden. Formerly a gamekeeper's cottage, it is believed that its name derives from the stone-mason who was responsible for the upkeep of the walls surrounding the Hall. There is a fine specimen of a lime kiln, now used as a garden store.

When you reach the lane of Winscombe Hill, turn right.

This area is an ideal place to park cars and garage services are available at Shute Shelve on the A38. There is no accommodation locally, but this and camping and caravanning are within the general area.

Horse-riders near King's Wood with Shute Shelve Hill beyond.

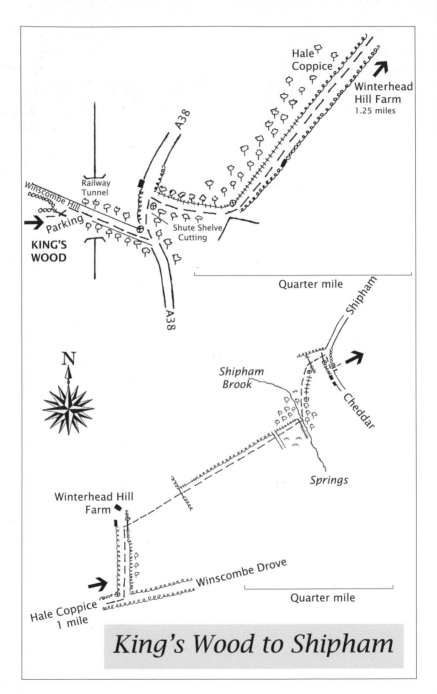

Hale
Coppice

Winterhead
Hill Farm
1.25 miles

A38

Railway
Tunnel

Winscombe Hill

Parking

**KING'S
WOOD**

Shute Shelve
Cutting

A38

Quarter mile

Shipham

Shipham
Brook

Cheddar

N

Springs

Winterhead Hill
Farm

Winscombe Drove

Hale Coppice
1 mile

Quarter mile

King's Wood to Shipham

4 King's Wood to Shipham

Distance:	2.5 miles (4 kms)
Maps:	Opposite & OS Explorer 141
Map Reference:	422560
Going:	An uphill walk which levels out along Winscombe Drove and then a steep descent to Shipham Brook before the final climb to Shipham.

Just before the Bristol to Exeter road (A38), the hidden, disused and only tunnel of the former Cheddar Valley Railway is crossed.

This branch line was opened from Yatton to Cheddar in 1869 and in the following year it was extended to Wells. The East Somerset Railway was built from Witham to Shepton Mallet in 1858 and to Wells in 1862. By 1878 this whole route had become known as the Cheddar Valley, but more affectionately as the Strawberry Line. It carried passengers mainly to Bristol and Weston-super-Mare but the quarries provided the main freight traffic, with cheese, until the increase in milk production and strawberries. It survived until 1963 for passengers, and stone was transported eastwards until it finally closed in 1968. A part of the route has now re-opened as an established walk and cycle-way.

Turn left to Shute Shelve.

Pronounced locally as 'Shelf', it is known in old records as The Shute, referring to the great hollow or cutting. On the right is a bare rock face, gradually becoming overgrown, which has been considerably reduced in size due to successive road widening schemes, particularly in the 1850's. Before this the road ran through a narrow defile, and built on the crest of the rocky bluff, of which now only a part remains, was the 17th century gallows. When the capture and trial was ordered by King James II of the Duke of Monmouth's rebels after the unsuccessful attempt to dethrone him, resulting in the Battle of Sedgemoor in 1685, Judge Jeffreys, a most feared and hated man, was authorised to set up his assizes in various west country towns. One such trial was held at Axbridge and men found guilty were brought to this place, many of them in shackles, and after being hanged, drawn and quartered, their remains were soaked in boiling pitch and then hung up to be clearly seen by travellers to set an example. The gruesome remains were said to have been buried on the spot, giving it the name of the Hanging Field. Other executions took place in later years and even sheep stealing remained a capital offence until 1832 when the penal laws were reformed.

Turn right opposite the garage and follow the track uphill on the northern edge of Rose Wood and around the northern flank of Shute Shelve Hill. At an obvious junction of footpaths, keep to the left.

This is Winscombe Drove, one of many dozens of ancient sheep-walks that are abundant on Mendip, used for the movement of sheep to market. These drove roads might have been established by the Celts in pre-Roman times but they certainly date from the Middle Ages and were used not only for sheep and packhorses but also by gypsies, pedlars and traders of all descriptions.

After about 1.25 miles (2 kms) from Shute Shelve turn left towards Winterhead Hill Farm. (Beware – do not take the first unmarked track to the left). Turn right just before the buildings, cross the field to the stile in a north-east

The Hanging Field at Shute Shelve, former site of the gallows.

The tree-lined and muddy Winscombe Drove.

> *direction and then keep the hedge on the left and descend the steep valley to Shipham Brook.*

To the right is the source from which Winscombe Brook forms the Lox Yeo River and the immediate area can be muddy or waterlogged.

> *Cross this little bubbling stream by the bridge. A steep climb is encountered and the road is reached at a height of over 500 feet (152 metres) on the southern edge of Shipham. Turn right for a few steps and, with extreme caution, cross the road.*

This road was one of many Mendip turnpike roads and was formed and administered by the Wedmore Trust in 1827. It provided a link from Pedwell, between Glastonbury and Taunton, through Wedmore and Cheddar to meet the Bristol to Bridgwater road near Rowberrow. These toll roads were introduced because of industrial expansion and the need for better connections within an increasingly affluent society. The cost of maintenance was reaped from the tolls collected at the gates and toll-bars from the road users themselves and not from the parish as beforehand. Up to the 18th century the roads were in a terrible state of repair and to travel by horse and carriage was very slow and not to be recommended as it was indeed quite dangerous.

The first trust to be established in North Somerset was the Bath Trust in 1707-1708. The Bristol Trust was formed in 1727 and was responsible for 69 miles of roads in Somerset, including the A38 at Shute Shelve, and the Wells Trust appeared in 1753. Next in this area came the Wedmore Trust in 1827, and then the Wells and Highbridge was founded in 1841.

The popularity of the railways was responsible for the eventual closure of the turnpikes and for the loss of custom at the coaching inns. The Bristol Trust was the first to suffer in 1867 and then came the Wells and Highbridge in 1870. The Wedmore Trust closed in 1874, the Bath Trust in 1878 and then the Wells in 1883. In an act of 1888 the county council was established as the statutory highway authority with responsibility for the roads within its territory. Some evidence of the turnpike era is still in existence in Shipham with its charming little tollhouse just beyond the village centre.

The earliest and most important industry around here was agriculture, reflected by the translation of the Anglo-Saxon names of *Ship*, meaning sheep, and *Ham* meaning an enclosure or farm. Known as *Sipeham* in the Domesday Book the present spelling of Shipham dates to about 1300. After the Roman decline and evacuation in 410 AD the Anglo-Saxons occupied

The Shipham tollhouse of 1827.

the area by the latter half of the 7th century and influenced the character of the villages, introducing field divisions, village names and local dialect. In the 13th century agriculture was becoming of secondary importance compared with mining, due to wars, crop failures and then the bubonic plague in the 14th century, so many of the manors became neglected and deserted. Sheep farming was, however, popular by the 15th century and an act of parliament in 1678 encouraged the manufacture of woollen materials when it became law that woollen shrouds had to be used for burials – an attempt to reduce the importation of foreign linen. The growth of manufactured sheepskin rugs, gloves and slippers in the early 19th century also contributed to this demand.

Mining was the next most successful industry, reaching a peak in the 18th century when almost all of the inhabitants of Shipham were digging. Nearly a hundred mines were evident in the fields, in the streets, and even in people's own backyards. Lead, calamine, manganese, zinc, iron, copper and ochre have been dug within these hills and small quantities of silver were also discovered. Coal was mined on Mendip in vast quantities up to 1973 but confined to the eastern region. Shipham and nearby Rowberrow were particularly noted for the mining of calamine, vital for the brass and zinc industries in the 18th century. It was probably not worked before 1600 but when lead extraction declined in the 18th century calamine became more sought-after. During the harsh days of poverty, disease and unemployment, mining provided a reasonable income for determined workers but the war with France in 1793 had a disastrous effect on the livelihood of the community and the demand for calamine slumped.

Religion in the 18th century was at a low ebb and the villagers were without any education but their total ignorance and offensive manners did arouse some sympathy amongst educated people. John Wesley, the English evangelist and founder of Methodism, preached in Shipham in 1782 but it was another seven years before the turning point for Shipham and many other villages.

Shipham villagers and miners during the late 18th century were said to be more savage, depraved and wretched than anywhere else. William Wilberforce (who fought for the abolition of slavery) visited Cheddar cliffs in 1789. He was so shocked and appalled at the unkempt and neglected people of Cheddar that he appealed to Hannah More, with whom he was staying at Cowslip Green, near Wrington, to help and teach them, promising that he would arrange financial backing.

Hannah More, a playwright and one of five daughters of a headmaster of a small foundation school, toured the area with her sister Martha and the miserable plight and degradation of the people she met affected her deeply. She was so concerned for their welfare that she opened a children's school in Cheddar in 1789 and the following year in Shipham. Several other schools and women's clubs were opened during their dedicated and successful campaign. Education was also extended to the parents, though she did experience much opposition from the farming communities who feared that religion would be the ruination of agriculture.

There is a memorial window to Hannah More in the church of St. Leonard in Shipham. In 1842 this church replaced a smaller and earlier building but the only remains of that are the oak font cover which was cut from the former church door, the carved wood panel which now acts as a reredos behind the altar, and possibly the gargoyles on the tower. In the entrance beneath the tower is an interesting list of Rectors since 1328, also of the Bishops of Bath and Wells and the Sovereigns of England.

Next to the church is the mediaeval Manor House built in 1383. On the opposite side of the road is the Court House, entirely rebuilt in about 1890 to replace the original in which, it is said, Judge Jeffreys presided. Many Shipham miners joined the rebellious army of the Duke of Monmouth in 1685; of those captured some were sentenced to deportation to the West Indies, but one man, Jacob Trypp of Shipham, was hanged by order of Judge Jeffreys, probably at Shute Shelve.

Shipham has a post office, garage services, accommodation and camping and caravanning can be found in the area. Car parking is also possible – with consideration.

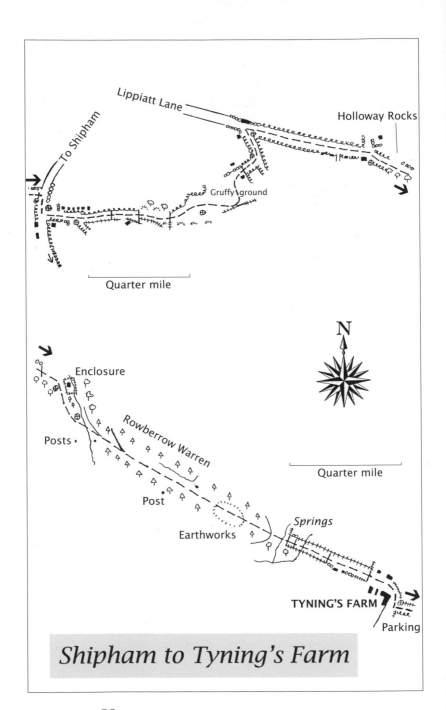

To Shipham

Lippiatt Lane

Holloway Rocks

Gruffy ground

Quarter mile

N

Enclosure

Rowberrow Warren

Posts ·

Post

Earthworks

Quarter mile

Springs

TYNING'S FARM

Parking

Shipham to Tyning's Farm

5 Shipham to Tyning's Farm

• •

Distance:	2.5 miles (4 kms)
Maps:	Opposite & OS Explorer 141
Map Reference:	443572
Going:	Mostly an uphill gradient to Holloway Rocks, a short descent into Rowberrow Bottom and then another gradual climb to Tyning's Farm.

From Cuck Hill, on the road south of the village, follow the lane beside the small green with the seat, ideal for a break, and continue along the track and signposted footpath. Any 'private' notices are not applicable for this footpath, a public right of way, so after the wicket gates follow the path through ferns and gorse to an area known as gruffy ground.

The pitted, scarred and uneven land is the result of the shallow diggings for minerals, the heaps being the waste material. The term 'gruffy' is a derivation of the word grooved. The free-miner was known as a 'groover' and his stake was claimed by standing in the waist-deep initially dug pit and throwing the lawfully recognised ten ounce 'hack', or pick, along a 'rake', or seam, as far as possible in either direction. This determined the boundaries of his land.

Two methods of finding minerals were employed. Since the veins were so rich and numerous a prospecting miner could just dig a trench until he came to a vein. Much faith, however, was placed in the second method, 'dowsing' or divining. Usually a Y-shaped piece of hazel or blackthorn, ten to twelve inches (25 to 31 centimetres) in length, would be used. With practice and a steady hand as much success was achieved as for the more common use in the search for water. The divining rod was in fact used for prospecting purposes before being used to locate water, and was introduced into England in about 1600 when German miners used it in the Welsh silver mines. 'Dowsing' continued throughout the mining era.

Theft from these workings did occur but the thief was never forgiven and was treated barbarously. He was pushed inside his building that was then set on fire and if he escaped he was expelled from the district forever.

Ancient customs and a code of mining laws for free-mining were made obsolete in 1795 when Mendip was enclosed by an act of parliament. The last miners to have worked this 'gruffy' ground has been recorded as 1853. Calamine was reduced to dust by being heated in ovens and the remains of just one oven still exist in Shipham.

On meeting the track bear left and right between the farm buildings to the gate. Follow the next track to the left that leads to Lippiatt Lane. Turn right and you are now following in the footsteps of the Roman legions again.

Hollow End, the last house on the right, was formerly three miner's cottages.

The route now descends through the cutting called The Holloway or Holloway Rocks.

It is possible that this little chasm is the 'Lippeat', or gate, from which the lane takes its name.

On entering Rowberrow Warren bear to the right of the Bristol Waterworks enclosure at Rowberrow Bottom.

This houses an 80,000 gallon (363,200 litres) underground reservoir and the water that feeds it is pumped from the

Above: Miners' 'Gruffy ground' at Shipham, last used in 1853.
Left: Old calamine oven in Shipham.

Rowberrow springs. The stream that flows alongside is from the Blackdown springs and is used only as a standby source when necessary. The stream, which can run at up to 130,000 gallons (590,000 litres) a day, continues along the valley and sinks into a number of 'swallets', or swallow-holes. 'Swallet' and 'slocker' are Mendip names which describe the point where a stream sinks underground through fissures in the limestone.

The path on the left leads to Dolebury Hill Fort, just over half a mile (1 km) and is well worth a visit. This is the largest and one of the finest examples on Mendip with its defensive ramparts still intact.

The path on the opposite side of the stream, also bearing left, is known as the 'Slaggers' Path and climbs the slopes of Blackdown; it was once used by the miners from Shipham. It is from near this point that the Limestone Link Path can be joined for the 36 miles (58 kms) to Cold Ashton which meets the Cotswold Way.

Follow the path to the right of the waterworks enclosure and cross the stream to take the uphill track through the plantation.

Left: Blackdown Springs in Rowberrow Bottom.
Right: Early 1900s identification post in Rowberrow Bottom.

Nearby are several iron posts, erected in the early 1900's, which probably marked the boundary of the water catchment area of the Axbridge Rural District Council. The springs were developed around 1899.

Rowberrow Warren was acquired by the Forestry Commission in 1937. The original bracken and shrub was replaced in 1941-48 with principally spruce but also larch, pine, Lawson's cypress and red cedar. In the spring of 1957 a fire destroyed 30% and 150 acres of this plantation, virtually across the whole width at this point. Conifers and beech were replanted during 1958-61 to replace the loss.

Follow the track and bridleway signs, still along the course of the Roman road.

Just before leaving the woods a pre-Roman earthworks is crossed. This is believed to be a communal burial ground and not of the tumulus type that was usually reserved for people of a high social position. The Romans had little respect for earlier settlements and built this road right through it.

Continue ahead to Tyning's Farm and Riding Centre.

The riding school is one of many in the area and can cater for the needs of visitors or regular riders alike. The bridleways around here are perfect for some peaceful and uninterrupted hacking.

Bear left and right through the farm to the lane.

Tyning's is a Saxon word meaning the enclosed or fenced fields and this farm is one of the oldest and most exposed on Mendip.

Opposite the farm entrance are the Tyning's Round Barrows, now rather overgrown and ploughed close to their edges. There are more than 300 Bronze Age tumuli on Mendip dating between c2,000 BC to c700 BC. Five here have been excavated and three proved to be earth burial mounds. Beneath one was found an urn containing the cremated remains of a woman and a child, a bronze awl, jet beads and green segmented faience beads. The other two barrows were surrounded by almost circular ditches and were constructed differently from each other. One contained a central ring cairn of old red sandstone blocks and was faced with upright limestone slabs whereas the other comprised stone cairns retained by outer kerbs.

Car parking is possible in a lay-by opposite the farm entrance. Accommodation is not available but camping and caravanning is found within the area.

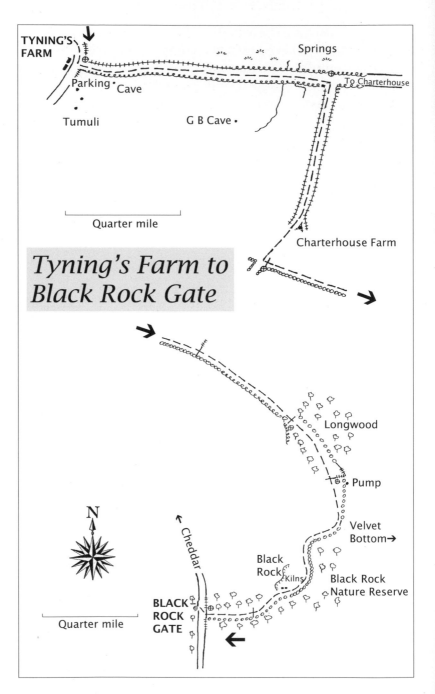

TYNING'S FARM

Parking · Cave

Tumuli

G B Cave ·

Springs

To Charterhouse

Quarter mile

Tyning's Farm to Black Rock Gate

Charterhouse Farm

Longwood

Pump

Velvet Bottom→

← Cheddar

Black Rock

Kilns

Black Rock Nature Reserve

BLACK ROCK GATE

N

Quarter mile

6 Tyning's Farm to Black Rock Gate

Distance:	3 Miles (4.8 kms)
Maps:	Opposite & OS Explorer 141
Map Reference:	470565
Going:	From the highest point of the West Mendip Way it is a gradual descent of easy walking, except for the section of stony path through Long Wood.

Turn left to take the lane east towards Charterhouse.

In the field on the right, by the stile, is a depression containing the entrance shaft to Tyning's Barrows Swallet, exposed when the storm and flood of 10th July, 1968 caused the depression floor to collapse. The length of the cave is over three-quarters of a mile (1.2 kms) and the total depth is 433 feet (132 metres).

The Roman road that is still being followed reaches the West Mendip Way's highest altitude at 870 feet (265 metres).

On the right, further along, is a field gate set back from the lane with a notice board declaring the Somerset Wildlife Trust's GB Gruffy Nature Reserve. The gruffy ground, almost due south, hides from view the entrances to several other caves, the most important and largest being GB Cave with its entrance covered by a concrete blockhouse. At present there are approximately one and a quarter miles (2 kms) of explored passages, reaching a total depth of 440 feet (134 metres). This is one of the caver's most popular caves in the Mendip Hills and its spectacular main chamber is the largest known chamber under them. Access is controlled as with many other caves on Mendip. The only tourist caves are at Cheddar and Wookey

Hole; many of the others need permission and perhaps a key to enter, specialised equipment and experience to explore.

The footpath turns right into the entrance to Charterhouse Farm and to Piney Sleight Farm.

The isolated and scattered community of Charterhouse is 1.25 miles (2kms) further along the road. Surrounded by prehistoric and Roman remains it derives its name from La Chartreuse, near Grenoble in France. In the 12th century the first Carthusian monastery was established at Witham Friary and monks from there were granted a charter by Henry II to start mining and grazing on land where a priory was built. This is said to be on the site now occupied by the 17th century Manor Farm in Charterhouse. The area was mined well over a thousand years before the monks came and, together with Priddy, was probably the most important and lucrative centre of lead mining. The heaviest pig of lead found in Britain was at Charterhouse in 1873 and weighed 223 lbs (101 kg). It bore the inscription of the Emperor Caesar Antoninus Augustus Pius.

Bear to the right of the farm bungalow, cross the field, turn left before the gate and follow the wall on the right-hand side with southerly views of the cliffs above Cheddar Gorge.

To the north is the heather-clad and bleak summit of Beacon Batch on Blackdown; at 1,068 feet (325 metres) above sea level it is the highest point of the Mendip Hills. There are several tumuli dotted around on the hillside and also retained are the concrete pillars, camouflaged with grass, erected during the Second World War to prevent enemy aircraft from landing. The receiving and transmitting masts in the north-east belong to a private wireless station.

From the corner of the field descend the stony path along the edge of Long Wood.

This wood has survived from Saxon times and contains many species of tree or bush which grow well in this sheltered hollow, including oak, beech, sycamore, field maple, ash, elder, sallow, spindle, hazel, hawthorn, blackthorn and dogwood. Mainly a broad-leaved woodland, it is a nature reserve and leased by the Somerset Wildlife Trust from the Bristol Waterworks Company. In the valley, approached from the south, are three caves, the largest of which is the Longwood/ August series. This cave is in excess of one mile (1.6 kms) in length and more than 574 feet (175 metres) in depth.

As you cross the stile into Black Rock Drove, a most delightful valley, note the disused iron water pump on the left, now without a handle, which has a date of 1884. Velvet Bottom, also leased to the Somerset Wildlife Trust from the Bristol Waterworks Company, is designated a Site of Special Scientific Interest and a diversion along this valley, especially by the industrial archaeologist or historian, could prove very rewarding.

Lead was mined extensively amongst this desolate landscape of heather and gorse until about 1830. It was first mined about 300 BC and it is believed that one of the main reasons for the Roman Invasion of 43 AD was the attraction of Mendip lead. After the withdrawal of the legions by Emperor Honorius in 410 AD it is not known if the Saxons worked these mines, although lead was used in their churches. Mining undoubtedly continued for some centuries, with charters being granted to the monastic communities, but information is rather scarce until the 16th or 17th century. Slag or refuse heaps along this valley are the results of re-smelting that took place since the 1820's which, because of the crude and wasteful methods employed in earlier times, gave a new lease of life to this industry until about 1875.

Above: Tyning's Farm and adjacent Bronze Age Round Barrows.

Below: Through Long Wood to Black Rock Drove.

Black Rock Nature Reserve is passed on the left and that also is managed by the Somerset Wildlife Trust under an agreement with the National Trust and with support from the Countryside Commission. It comprises 121 acres of plantation, mixed natural woodland, scrub, rough downland and scree. Many of the trees visible from the drove are Scots pine and larch; the latter is Britain's only common conifer that in winter loses its needles.

The yellowhammer is frequently seen in this neighbourhood, the male being the brightest yellow bird in Britain, and the greater butterfly orchid and the common spotted orchid grow underfoot in the short turf.

Black Rock Quarry takes its name from the dark grey and fine-grained limestone that was extracted from here from the mid-1920's for only about ten years. A good example of the limestone strata can be studied showing the vertical fissures that allow rainwater to seep through and forms, over many thousands of years, caves. Lime kilns were probably constructed towards the end of the 18th century when lime was used in vast quantities on the fields to replace the washed-away natural lime on sloping land. Limestone was heated with coal or wood, dowsed with water, and the lumps transported to the fields to be crushed to powder. It was also used as a mortar for the building of walls.

When you reach the road at Black Rock Gate the village of Cheddar is almost two miles (3.2 kms) downhill to the right, at the foot of Cheddar Gorge. This is one of the most dramatic natural features in England, but the formation of this spectacular and breath-taking canyon is still the cause of scientific conjecture. This winding road was built in 1801 and the sheer wall of rock above reaches a height of 450 feet (137 metres) in places and the rock ledges and tiny clefts offer a perfect environment and adequate protection for some very rare plants. The Cheddar Pink (*Dianthus gratianopolitanus*) is of major importance as it is native in Britain only in Cheddar Gorge. Various other rare plants and ferns attract the botanist

Above: Black Rock Drove.

Below: The disused quarry at Black Rock.

The soaring limestone cliffs at Cheddar Gorge.

(for study only) as well as the more familiar figure of the climber and caver. I have myself explored the majority of almost four dozen caves in the vicinity of the gorge and directed an excavation of a small cave that revealed bones of extinct animals from the Pleistocene period (1-2 million years BC). There are also many traces of human occupation in some of the caves in the shape of bones, tools, flint weapons, iron spearheads, bronze ornaments, pottery and hundreds of Roman coins. The main inhabitants now are spiders and various species of bats including the greater and lesser horseshoe bats.

Only two significant caves are open to the public and the first cave opened for commercial gain was the one discovered by Richard Gough in 1877, now known as Gough's Old Cave. When the larger cavern was revealed by digging in 1893 the original was then closed and the public admitted to this, the largest of the Cheddar caves, in 1900. Three years later the skeleton of a primitive cave dweller was discovered in a fissure.

Radiocarbon dated to c7130 BC, and known as Cheddar Man, it is exhibited with finds from the Palaeolithic age (c60,000 BC) in the cave's museum. Cox's Cave, discovered in 1837, is smaller but considered to be more decorative with some very beautiful formations. The River Yeo, or Cheddar Water, has been traced from springs and then to swallets in the Charterhouse and Long Wood areas, eventually flowing out from Gough's Cave below the cliff face and into the lake opposite.

The name of Cheddar is said to derive from the Celtic *Ced*, meaning a cliff or height, and *Dwr*, possibly meaning water. The first known reference, to the brethren and sisters at Cheddar Minster, appeared in a charter of King Edgar in 998 AD. The Normans in the Domesday Book refer to it as *Cedre*.

The site of the palace or residence of Saxon kings was discovered in 1962 during the digging of foundations for the King's of Wessex Upper School. Excavations and detailed surveys proved to archaeologists that the earliest period of occupation was during the 9th century as coins and animal bones of that date were found. The excavated area forms a large sunken frontage to the school's entrance. The stone chapel of St. Columbanus has stood on this site since c930 AD but has been rebuilt and the present ruin dates from the 13th century. In 1999, whilst excavating for a new classroom, a 3rd or 4th century Roman barn was discovered.

Nearby, in Lower North Street, is Hannah More's first school of 1789, originally thatched, now used by the parish council. The Cheddar Cross dates from two separate periods. The inner preaching cross is 15th century but the outer roof and arches were erected in 1887, replacing the 16th century original.

The splendid church of St. Andrew, the fourth known to have been build here, was completed between 1380-1480. The lofty but graceful perpendicular tower rises in three stages to 110 feet (33.5 metres), incorporating, it is said, bricks from a nearby Roman villa. The open parapets and slender pinnacles are also most admirable. In the churchyard, under the sycamore tree to the south, is the grave of the hymn-writer William Chatterton Dix (1837-1898) whose best-known hymn was 'As with gladness men of old'. Inside, the gilded and painted roof is a most interesting feature and there is rich woodwork in the carved bench ends. The font is early 14th century and the cover is Jacobean, or early 17th century. Some stained glass dates from the 1470's and the richly carved 15th century stone pulpit is another of the finest examples in Somerset.

Somerset cheese has a history dating to 1170 but probably the earliest mention of Cheddar cheese was in the 1560's. William Camden writes of cheese making around Cheddar in his famous work *Britannia* of 1586 and in 1724 Daniel Defoe said that it was probably the best cheese in England and that almost every villager kept cows. A story is told that cheese was produced accidentally after an absent-minded milkmaid left a pail of milk in a cave for a few hours and without any doubt it has become famous and popular throughout the world.

Cheddar is an excellent centre for the Mendip Hills, with shops, accommodation, camping and caravanning sites, parking and garage facilities.

Cheddar Gorge.

73

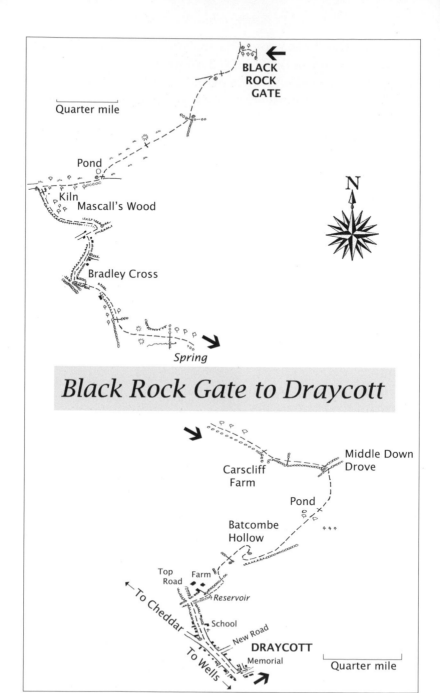

Quarter mile

BLACK ROCK GATE

Pond

Kiln

Mascall's Wood

Bradley Cross

N

Spring

Black Rock Gate to Draycott

Middle Down Drove

Carscliff Farm

Pond

Batcombe Hollow

Top Road

Farm

To Cheddar

Reservoir

School

New Road

DRAYCOTT

To Wells

Memorial

Quarter mile

74

7   Black Rock Gate
to Draycott

Distance:	3.5 miles (5.6 kms)
Maps:	Opposite & OS Explorer 141
Map Reference:	482545
Going:	A steep climb from Cheddar Gorge to the top of the cliffs, downhill to Bradley Cross, ascending again above Carscliff Farm and then downhill to Draycott.

Almost directly across the Cheddar George road follow the rocky uphill path.

Shaded and bordered by hazel, ash, birch, whitebeam and yew, this path lifts the walker to the gorse-covered and exposed downland that attracts a wide variety of birds and butterflies.

Go through the gate and then bear left (where another wider and more prominent path leads to the right). The West Mendip Way then meets a wall to the left and ahead. Cross the stile in the corner and bear away from the wall again and continue downhill with the tower above Jacob's Ladder, Cheddar and the reservoir ahead.

The almost circular reservoir, built in 1938, is three-quarters of a mile (1.2 kms) in diameter. With a storage capacity of 1,300 million gallons (5,910 million litres), it is fed by the springs at the foot of the hills and is popular for dinghy sailing and coarse fishing. Freshwater ducks make up the largest concentration of waterfowl with some occasional and very rare visitors.

The dewpond to the right of the path, the circular stone-built shallow depression from which farm animals drink, is thought to have been built at the time of the Enclosure Acts in the late 18th century. The Saxons probably introduced the divisions of estates on the Mendip plateau but from the mid-16th century private ownership brought further boundaries. Agricultural development was encouraged in the 18th century and the characteristic dry limestone walls began to appear. Stone was used as the cheapest and most available material on the main plateau, but hedgerows are more common on Eastern Mendip. John Billingsley (1747-1811) of Ashwick Grove, near Oakhill, was credited with the improvement and enclosure of Mendip after his agricultural survey of 1795.

In Mascall's Wood, owned by the Somerset Wildlife Trust, the remains of the boundary-marking bank and ditch date from prehistoric days, but the walls were built within the last 200 years or so.

Keep the broken wall on the left and turn left at the western edge of the wood.

The lime kiln, on the left, was certainly built before 1880 and was used for producing the lime for the walls. It is of an unusual design and very rare on Mendip and the stone came from a very small quarry in the woods. There are about twenty species of trees and shrubs that include oak, ash, field maple, wych elm, beech, whitebeam, wild cherry, spindle, privet, holly and yew.

Take the path on the left, alongside the kiln, keeping the hedgerow on the right and at the path junction turn right and then left. Continue along the lane and just before Bradley Cross Lane turn left along the track and into the field. Start climbing and then a shaded path is followed until open downland is reached and southerly views appear.

Above: Cheddar and the reservoir, with Brent Knoll beyond and Axbridge, Crook Peak and Wavering Down to the right.

Below: Dewpond above Batcombe Hollow near Draycott.

This area is frequented by buzzards, sometimes three or four together, gliding through the air with a slow flapping of broad wings and a mewing call. This large bird of prey with its sharp eyes will pounce on a victim as small as a beetle but will itself be mobbed sometimes by crows. When this happens the buzzard will usually face its tormentors with its sharp talons.

The path curves eastwards, keeping to the ridge of the hill and between two low embankments to a gate.

The trough here is fed by springs, and some of the water is pumped into a storage tank for use at nearby Carscliff farm.

Continue uphill along the track beneath the avenue of oak, ash, field maple and hawthorn with the broken wall on the right with its unsightly repair of corrugated iron sheets and wire fencing. At the farm junction keep ahead and uphill until the footpath reaches more exposed grazing land and the best view of Axbridge on the far side of the reservoir.

So important was this Saxon market town and fortress to the royal palace at Cheddar that it even supported a mint that produced coins from 997 to 1042. The name Axbridge probably means the burgh or township overlooking the River Axe and not on the banks, a mile to the south. The church of St. John the Baptist is now almost entirely in the perpendicular style of the 15th century with its grand central tower of the Cheddar Valley type. From the square, where bull baiting was held well into the 19th century, is the narrow High Street lined with many ancient houses and shops. The most famous is the inaptly-named King John's Hunting Lodge. This well-preserved mediaeval timber-framed building, with protruding upper storeys, was built in about 1490 as a merchant's house incorporating three shops. In the 17th and 18th centuries it was known as the King's Head Alehouse with the carved oak head of King John probably being used as the inn-sign. King John, who reigned from 1199 to 1216, obviously never stayed here but probably at Cheddar where royalty had their palaces. It is believed, however, that a Saxon hunting lodge may have existed at Axbridge, perhaps even on this site. This house, now owned by the National Trust, is also the town's museum. One of the more recent discoveries in the town exhibited here is a Roman skeleton unearthed in 1982. The body was buried wearing hob-nailed boots and some nails and pieces of leather have remained intact. It was at Axbridge, in about 1870, that strawberries – a speciality of the area – were first grown, and then later at Cheddar.

Cross Middle Down Drove and bear in a southerly direction towards a group of thinly planted but tall pine trees, with the view of Draycott ahead. Keeping these on the left, and the dew pond on the right, follow the developing rutted track between a pair of hawthorn trees and continue downhill.

This stretch overlooks many acres of strawberry fields, the former course of the Cheddar Valley railway and Nyland Hill. In the south-south-east is the 521 feet (159 metres) high Glastonbury Tor, dominating the surrounding lowlands and crowned with the 14th century tower of a ruined church dedicated to St. Michael.

Steeped in legend and history, Glastonbury is the cradle of Christianity in the British Isles with the first church being built by Joseph of Arimathea on his arrival from the Holy Land in about 30-32 AD. He planted his staff on the slopes of Wearyall Hill; it took root and flowered and from it was taken many cuttings. Some descendants of this Glastonbury Thorn still survive; one grows in the abbey grounds, and another in the churchyard of St. John's, whose tower you can also see. The cup used at the Last Supper, the Holy Grail, which, it is reputed, contained droplets of Christ's blood, was supposedly buried

Above: Batcombe Hollow above Draycott.

Left: Draycott water pump.

at the foot of the Tor, by Joseph, at the site of the Chalice Well, a place consequently noted for its healing powers.

It is said that, prior to this, Joseph was a merchant trading in Mendip lead, and that on at least one of his missions to Priddy he was accompanied by Jesus, then in his early 'teens. Perhaps William Blake's early 19th century poem 'Jerusalem' has a measure of truth in the lines – 'And did those feet in ancient time, walk upon England's mountains green'.

The first monastic foundation in England was built through a charter of King Ina in 688 AD, but a fire in 1184 destroyed Joseph's wattle church and the majority of the abbey buildings. Rebuilding of the great abbey resulted in the richest and most influential in England and this was one of the last to fall, in 1539, at the time of the dissolution of the monasteries.

The last abbot, Richard Whiting, was sentenced to death in the great hall of the Bishop's Palace in Wells on an invented charge of robbery against the church as he refused to surrender the abbey to Henry VIII. He was dragged to the top of the Tor and hanged, drawn and quartered. The abbey became a ruin and some of the stone was used to build a road across the marshes to Wells.

Glastonbury, or the romantically linked Isle of Avalon, is reputed to be the last resting-place for Joseph, St. Patrick, and the legendary King Arthur with his Queen Guinevere. With his Knights of the Round Table, Arthur (492-542 AD) had his hill-top Camelot Castle at South Cadbury, a little further to the south-east.

In the distance between the trees, beyond and to the right of the Tor and almost to the south, is the Hood Monument, in memory of Sir Samuel Hood, Baronet and Commander-in-chief of his Majesty's fleet in the East Indies.

Follow the bend into Batcombe Hollow, cross the stile and then follow the wall on the right alongside the farm buildings.

The farmhouse was built in c1500 by Abbot Richard Bere of Glastonbury as a meeting house and the second-floor hall is now divided into separate rooms.

On reaching Top Road turn left; it becomes School Lane, leading you into the village of Draycott, and passes the school and St. Peter's Church (1861) on the left.

Opposite and on the corner of the main road (A371) is an old stone pillar with an iron frame from which used to hang a paraffin lamp. It was last used in about 1914. The Methodist chapel on the corner of New Road was built in 1876, replacing an earlier one of c1820 further up New Road, but both are now unused as chapels. After passing the Red Lion public house, four cottages higher up on the left are the former stables, cutting and polishing plant of Bryscombe Quarry, closed down in about 1939.

Many buildings, walls and gate-posts were built with the local dolomitic conglomerate (commonly known as pudding-stone) which has been quarried here since Saxon days. The reddish tinge of the fragmented rock provides an attractive contrast to the light colour of the more commonly used Doulting limestone. Draycott 'marble' was a speciality that can be found in many buildings, including St. Peter's Church, Loxton Parish Church, Wedmore Church and Wells Cathedral. The stone was cut by a carborundum saw, with sand and water being used as lubricants, polished with pumice stone and finally with putty powder to produce a glossy surface like that of marble. This 'marble' was produced possibly as early as the 13th century (four polished columns were erected at the western end of the nave in Wells Cathedral), but more certainly by 1660 when the west front was restored.

The Card Memorial commemorates John Card of Draycott, who founded the Draycott Charity by donating much land to the villagers. The rent collected was distributed amongst the 'second' poor, and the trust still continues. Card, who died in

1729 and is buried in Cheddar churchyard, left a request that at each AGM of the charity the committee should eat, drink and smoke to his memory. The plinth of the monument came from Watt's Quarry, which closed in 1917, but the obelisk is of Aberdeen granite. The village pump nearby was last used in the early 1970's and is now preserved for posterity.

Mentioned in the Domesday Book as *Draicote*, the village was originally a hamlet belonging to Rodney Stoke, but became an ecclesiastical parish in 1862. The former station buildings of the Cheddar Valley railway still survive, now converted into a private dwelling. The only industry now remaining is market gardening, with strawberries being the main crop.

A post office and general stores can be found in The Street and overnight accommodation might be possible. Car parking can be found, especially on enquiry, with the usual consi-deration.

The Card Memorial in Draycott.

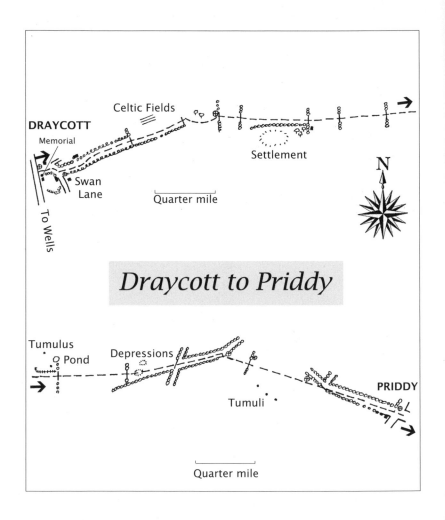

Celtic Fields

DRAYCOTT

Memorial

Swan
Lane

To Wells

Settlement

N

Quarter mile

Draycott to Priddy

Tumulus
Pond   Depressions

Tumuli

PRIDDY

Quarter mile

8 Draycott to Priddy

Distance:	3 miles (4.8 kms)
Maps:	Opposite & OS Explorer 141
Map Reference:	477510
Going:	A steep uphill gradient for over a mile (1.6kms) to the second highest point, then levelling out generally with a slight descent to Priddy.

From the Card Memorial walk uphill along The Batch, bear right and then left along Sun Batch. (The face of the disused Watt's Quarry can be seen from Swan Lane to the right.) After passing strawberry fields the very steep lane deteriorates into a track. Cross the stone stile and keep the field boundary to the right.

To the left, on the slopes of Draycott Hill overlooking the valley, known locally as Draycott Steep, there is evidence of Celtic terraced field cultivation.

Cross the rocky outcrop and continue over the hill in an almost easterly direction to the stone stile. Take note that some of the stone stiles in this vicinity have been painted yellow to aid navigation. Cross the next stile in the same direction to meet the wall on your right.

On the other side, on the brow of the hill, is a Celtic hill settlement believed to have been used in the Iron Age from c700 BC.

Here, the West Mendip Way is at its second highest point, at about 863 feet (263 metres). Of all sections, this 720 feet

Cultivated fields at Draycott.

Draycott Steep.

Typical Mendip drystone wall and stile above Draycott.

(219 metres) climb from Draycott is the greatest. To the left, and north, across the valley, is the airfield at Halesland used as a gliding school and by the Air Training Corps. On the right is Westbury Beacon, used by hang-gliders as a taking-off point.

Cross the stile at the corner near the tall beech, ash, oak and sycamore trees. Cross the next three fields, heading towards the east, and to the far distant tumuli but to the left of a group of beech trees on the far side of the third field; alongside a wire enclosure to the stile.

There are more tumuli on the left, one being close and visible. Nearby, but out of sight, is a dewpond. The distant view of North Hill beyond Priddy shows the shape of two sets of round barrows of the Bronze Age period of about 2,000-700 BC. These comprise Priddy Nine Barrows on the right and another group of eight, known as Ashen Hill Barrows, to the left. Combined, these constitute one of the finest examples in England. They were excavated by the Rev. John Skinner of Camerton in 1815 and he discovered many relics. Many sites of antiquity, particularly these burial mounds around Priddy, were opened in his search for valuables and these were sold to boost his church funds.

Keep straight ahead to meet the wall, passing two shallow depressions, and continue to the road. Follow the lane opposite, Coxton End Lane, for less than 400 yards (366 metres) until a slight bend. Turn right into the field and head across the centre to the next field. Cross the stile and with three tumuli on the right, head east with the shallow depressions also on the immediate right. As the land begins to rise bear left to the gate and stile. Turn right along The Batch, with views to the Old Rectory, the church of St. Lawrence and another, better, view of North Hill, to reach Priddy Green.

Stone stile between Draycott and Priddy.

Priddy Church on the left and North Hill with Priddy Nine Barrows on the right.

St. Lawrence Church, Priddy.

Situated in a shallow hollow on the high plateau at about 800 feet (244 metres) Priddy is, in winter, one of the bleakest and most isolated Mendip villages. It is said to have taken its name from the Welsh *Pridd*, meaning earth or soil, and although mentioned in a Saxon charter it was not recorded in the Domesday Book. The church of St. Lawrence was dedicated in 1352 and is set within a large expanse of neatly trimmed churchyard. Of interest is the 13th century tower; 11th century font; late 15th century tapestry and the late 15th century rood screen.

When the Black Death, or bubonic plague, of the 14th century spread from Europe and engulfed the cities and towns of southern England it is believed that an annual sheep fair was moved from Wells to the healthier climate of the hills. To escape the dreaded pestilence, in 1348, the fair was installed on the triangular Priddy Green and attracted sheep farmers and dealers in other animals, together with gypsies, tinkers and pedlars. This has been the venue every August since that time and the fair and auction is held on the Wednesday nearest to the 21st. Since those days when sheep were driven along the drove roads, animals are now transported by lorries and modern side-shows and roundabouts have taken the place of the boxing booth and cock-fighting pit. A reminder of those times is the thatched stack of wooden hurdles on the green that has stood here for 300 years but as they are decaying they are no longer used for the sheep enclosures.

This scattered village is a Mecca for cavers with the entrance to Swildon's Hole situated on private farmland just to the east of the church. This cave is the largest and most popular on Mendip with well over 5.5 miles (8.8 kms) of passages and a vertical range of 550 feet (168 metres). Names of various parts of the cave such as the Lavatory Pan, Abandon Hope, Mayday Passage, Sore Knees Creep and Fool's Paradise conjure up visions of danger and discomfort, but fit, experienced, cautious and well equipped teams may explore the cave's secrets safely and successfully. The stream entering Swildon's Hole is fed

The triangular Priddy Green.

from Priddy Pool, in Nine Barrows Lane (as marked on the O/S map), and is just one of the many sources of the River Axe.

From the early discovery of caves in the pursuit of archaeology and geology, the pattern of caving developed. From the original quest for scientific knowledge developed the modern and exciting sport of caving. The early pioneers paved the way for the cavers of today to explore as far as possible in our cave systems. With help from a pick or shovel, and the occasional careful and controlled use of explosives, huge caverns, miles of decorated passages, and many beautiful formations have been discovered. The Mendip Nature Research Club (now Committee) was the first caving club to be founded on Mendip in 1906, combining cave exploration with scientific study. The first cave-dive organised on Mendip took place in Swildon's Hole in 1934. This was with unreliable equipment but now the apparatus used is technically tested, well proven and dependable. Many dozens of caves exist on Mendip and a guidebook is available which details conditions of entry, cave route descriptions and tackle required.

Since the Romans mined lead, Priddy has for centuries been the centre of this industry over a large radius. The ruins of St. Cuthbert's leadworks, a mile (1.6 kms) to the east, still survive but are not visible from this footpath. So important was lead that it made Priddy and Charterhouse famous as the main producers of this valuable metal.

Wookey Hole paper mill complained that polluted water from the buddles, or washing places, of St. Cuthbert's works was being discharged into the streams and, after sinking underground into the 'swallets', was re-appearing at the mill. This not only affected the quality of the paper but also of the water supply to the villagers. A court action in 1863 resulted in the lead-works having to pump and re-use the water until it evaporated. This added to the work of the miners and the works closed in 1869. However, it re-opened ten years later and, whilst most of the other lead-works ceased work in about 1875, St. Cuthbert's remained in business until 1908, the last to close down. Priddy's only industry now is agriculture, reflecting the main occupation of these hills.

A plaque, by the roadside on the northern edge of Priddy Green, is sited where the first supply of pure water was given to the villagers in 1865 by James Green Esq., Lord of the Manor.

Accommodation could be limited but a camping and caravanning site is situated half a mile (0.8 kms) to the north-west of the village green and the site has a general store. The village post office has very limited opening times. There are no problems with car parking.

Thatched stack of wooden hurdles on Priddy Green.

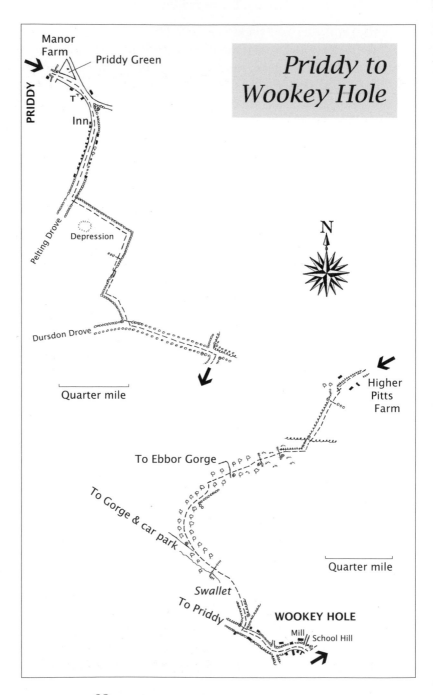

Priddy to Wookey Hole

Manor Farm

Priddy Green

PRIDDY

T

Inn

Pelting Drove

Depression

Dursdon Drove

N

Quarter mile

Higher Pitts Farm

To Ebbor Gorge

To Gorge & car park

Quarter mile

Swallet

To Priddy

WOOKEY HOLE

Mill
School Hill

9 Priddy to Wookey Hole

Distance:	3 miles (4.8 kms)
Maps:	Opposite & OS Explorer 141
Map Reference:	527509
Going:	A level walk to Ebbor Gorge Nature Reserve and then a steep descent before the level terrain to Wookey Hole.

With Priddy Green to the left, keep straight ahead with the New Inn on the right.

This building was originally a farmhouse and dates back to 1446. Opposite the stables is Pincross Cottage and the inscription on the wall is believed to have been written by the builder:

> This stone my name shall evar
> Have when I hame dead and laye
> in my grave and greedy wormes
> my body eat then you may read
> my name compleat.
> Thomas Reeves 1739

Bear to the right along Pelting Drove and pass the Queen Victoria Inn on the right.

This was so named in 1847, just ten years after the Queen's accession to the throne. The line of hawthorn trees on the left is most attractive when in full flower in June.

After almost half a mile (0.8 kms) cross the stile on the

left. Continue around the edge of this field in a clockwise direction, with the large depression on your right, and cross the stile in the corner furthermost from the road. Midway across the next field cross the stone stile in the wall on the left and then turn right. Follow the edge of this field in an anti-clockwise direction and cross the stile to join Dursdon Drove. Follow this to the left and turn right at the next track to Higher Pitts Farm.

The field on the right had a searchlight installation in the Second World War and is now known locally as Searchlight Field. This farm area was the scene of a thriving 18th century iron manufacturing industry but all that now remains are the former miners' cottages that have been converted into the farmhouse. The valley by Dursdon Wood, on the right, was known as Iron Pit Bottom and in the 1850's manganese was also mined but this ceased by the end of that decade. It re-started in 1890 and was the final short-lived attempt on Mendip at authentic mining (all other businesses were mainly employed with the re-smelting of refuse) but work ceased finally in 1891.

There was much scientific interest in the discovery of the rare mineral called Mendipite. It is maintained that 26 different minerals have been found here, and it is one of the very few places in the world where so many have been discovered in such a small area. Virtually all of the mine shafts have now been filled in but evidence still remains of some of their locations in small depressions.

Continue between the farm and the house and follow the directional arrows heading in a south-south-west direction to the field with the hedge on the right. At the next field bear to the right around the fence and away from the television transmitter.

Built in 1969 on the 1,002 feet (305.5 metres) summit of Pen

*Left: Pen Hill
television mast.*

*Below: An entrance
to the Ebbor Gorge
Nature Reserve.*

Hill, this is itself 1,000 feet (305 metres) in height with its platform at 910 feet (277 metres). It also has a lift, capable of carrying two people, for maintenance purposes. It transmits all terrestrial television channels and is used by over 30 other subscribers including public services such as police, ambulance, water, gas and electricity boards and by radio amateurs. Serving more than two million people in Somerset, North Devon, North Dorset, West Wiltshire and South Gloucestershire, it has 44 satellite transmitters based over a wide area.

Enter the Ebbor Gorge Nature Reserve, with extensive views in the south, and continue downhill along the track bearing to the left. At the junction in the woods go straight ahead.

The narrow, secluded and tree-shrouded Ebbor Gorge with the surrounding 116 acres of woodland, rock and scree was presented to the National Trust in 1967 by Mrs Olive Hodgkinson in memory of Sir Winston Churchill. Managed by English Nature, it is an unspoilt natural habitat for all forms of wildlife including buzzards, which have nested here, and there are active badger setts close to the footpath. Foxes, grey squirrels, rabbits, stoats, weasels, moles and voles are also common. Deer also inhabit the woods but are rarely seen. Ash, beech, pedunculate oak, wych elm and hazel form the bulk of the forestry growth and the ground cover includes wood sorrel, yellow archangel, travellers joy, birdsfoot trefoil, dogs mercury, bluebell, marsh marigold, nettles, ferns and numerous fungi. Also to be found here are the sparrowhawk, kestrel, green and great spotted woodpecker, jay, linnet, blackcap, stonechat, goldcrest, woodcock, owl and bat.

To reach the gorge turn right at the junction and, using extreme caution, negotiate the rocky and steep defile to reach the bottom. This tricky diversion should only be attempted if you are fit and athletic owing to the possible danger of an accident in this remote and hidden region. Pass the scree slope and the West Mendip Way can be rejoined by keeping straight ahead to the bottom of the steps on the left. (The path to the right continues through the woods and either path later will lead to the car park, display centre and picnic area high up on the hillside adjoining the Priddy to Wookey Hole road.) The walks and scrambles through Ebbor Gorge and the woods are both enchanting and delightful but a word of warning to the unwary: in hot summer weather adders are quite common, as elsewhere on Mendip, and they can bite. Grass snakes and slow worms are also numerous but these are harmless.

Bronze Age man of between 2,500 and 4,000 years ago once occupied the many small caves in this area and excavations have unearthed considerable numbers of bones, tools and cooking utensils. All these caves are now, however, filled in.

If keeping to the correct route without diverting to the gorge, continue straight ahead. At 50 yards (45 metres) before the cliff edge (a wonderful viewpoint) turn left and follow the steep descending path with over 100 steps cut into the hillside. This is particularly painful on sore feet or weary legs, and the climb from the opposite direction is very demanding indeed on the walker's fitness and stamina especially if you are carrying heavy rucksacks. At the bottom turn left.

(To reach Deerleep car park, take the path to the right and then left.)

Cross the boundary of the Nature Reserve and continue along level ground (but possibly very muddy) to the lane, Kennel Batch. Turn left.

Ebbor Hall Farm on the right was built in the late 17th century. The annexe to the right, Ebbor Hall cottages, and the stables, are more recent additions from 1925. Ebbor House opposite,

Above left: The Way through Ebbor Gorge Nature Reserve.
Above right: Looking back at the road-sign in Wookey Hole.

Below: Bubwith Farm and the River Axe with Wookey Hole paper
mill in the background.

formerly called Ebbor Cottage, a farm cottage, was built in the early 19th century and extended in the Victorian style in 1898. Just past the entrance to Ebborlands Riding Centre, also on the left, is Wookey House, built in 1720; the early Georgian front was added in about 1780. Around the bend is Pink Lodge, also of the same age as Wookey House and thought to have been the lodge or gardener's cottage to the estate.

Opposite are six cottages known as The Croft, built in 1902, originally mill workers' houses. Occupants of three have experienced strange happenings. There are reports of an occasional mysterious strong scent, all the more puzzling because the last three dogs owned by the occupiers became agitated and alarmed until the scent dispersed. In another house had lived an old lady with a club foot who walked with the aid of a stick. Even after she died, neighbours heard her going upstairs and downstairs, the sound of her crippled progress on the bare stair-boards quite unmistakable.

An even more remarkable story concerns another old lady, white-haired, who died in the house in the mid-1950's. Families who lived in the house afterwards reported that this lady was still to be seen at the top of the stairs. One morning a little girl asked her mother who was the white-haired lady who had tucked her up in bed the previous night. Eventually a former Bishop of Bath and Wells performed a rite of exorcism and since then no further sightings have been spoken of.

On the same side of the road, situated almost opposite and just beyond the path for Wookey Hole Cave, is Bubwith Farm, the oldest building in Wookey Hole. It dates from the early 15th century during the office of Bishop Bubwith of Wells, from whom it takes its name. It ceased working as a farm in 1927.

Wookey Hole village is said to take its name from Celtic times with the name of *Wocob* or *Wocov* meaning a hole or cave. In 1586 William Camden, one of the founders of English historiography, produced *Ochie*, and this later developed into the word as it is now known. 'Hole' was added to differentiate between this village and Wookey, two miles to the south-west.

The great cave of Wookey Hole, which is open to the public, is approached by walking along the lovely wooded valley alongside the River Axe. The emergence of this river from the mouth of the cave has encouraged many water tracings to probe the secret of its source. Hydrologists have proved that the River Axe is fed by several 'swallets' higher up on the Mendip plateau, including Swildon's Hole, but have little knowledge of the mysterious and lengthy underground course that disgorges to sunlight as the second largest river on Mendip. Cave divers have now discovered 25 chambers but only the early ones are accessible to visitors. The total length, including submerged passageways, is now in excess of two miles (3.2 kms) and exploration continues.

Celtic tribes occupied the cave from about 250 BC for perhaps 300 years, and many bones, tools, weapons and other implements have been found. The skeleton of a woman was discovered, together with a stalagmitic ball and other relics, resulting in the well-known legend of the Witch of Wookey. The most popular belief is that in the 15th century a woman recluse lived in the cave and cast spells on the young maidens of the village and performed other evil deeds. The villagers appealed to the Abbot of Glastonbury and a young monk was sent to the cave. He scooped up some water from the underground River Axe, blessed it, and poured this holy water over the woman, turning her to stone.

Badger Hole, one of four small caves in the ravine, has revealed traces of civilisation very much earlier than the great cave, back in fact to the Old Stone Age of about 25,000 years ago. Remains of extinct animals of as long ago as 60,000 years have also been found in these caves and these are exhibited in the cave museum and at Wells Museum.

The paper mill was Somerset's earliest mill and records show that paper was being manufactured there as early as 1610. There was possibly a mill on this site as far back as the 11th century, but then it probably produced corn or cloth. The invention of printing in the 15th century encouraged the manufacture of paper, and many mills were converted to this use. This mill was ideally situated with the river Axe emerging fast flowing and pure, except in the times of lead pollution as mentioned previously.

In a fire of 1855 it was destroyed but the mill re-opened in 1858 and the present frontage to the building was completed in 1900. It always had a fine reputation for good quality handmade paper, including foreign banknote paper, and this was produced commercially until 1972 when the mill closed down. Competition from machine-made paper at very competitive prices was too great a challenge for this highly skilled and ancient craft. St. Cuthbert's mill at Haybridge, half a mile (0.8 kms) along the river, is now the only survivor of the Mendip paper-making industry.

The cave and mill complex is open to the public, almost every day of the year, and the buildings now house a variety of entertainment, finds from the caves, and paper-making equipment. The owners of the mill since 1848 were the Hodgkinson family, the principal employers and benefactors of the village. They built houses for the workers, the school (1872), the village club (1884) and St. Mary Magdalene Church (1887).

Most of the stone used in the building of Wookey Hole village came from Hole Ground up and beyond School Hill. Once levelled for the school playing field (the school is now a nursing home), it was a quarry, and a short section of metal rail that was used to haul the stone can still be seen. A Roman villa was built nearby, according to the findings of archaeologists.

Accommodation in Wookey Hole is limited, but camping and caravanning facilities are available in and near the village. There is a post office and general stores but no garage services exist and car parking is very restricted, particularly in the summer season. The large car park with the restaurant and tourist gift shop belongs to the cave management and is for the use of visitors to the cave and these other amenities.

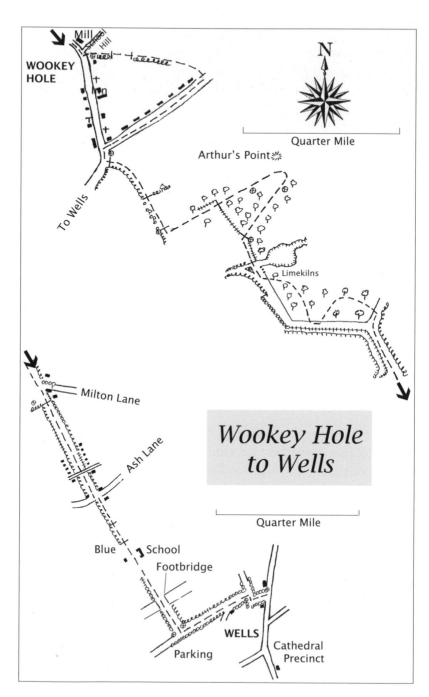

N

Quarter Mile

WOOKEY HOLE

Mill Hill

Arthur's Point

To Wells

Limekilns

Milton Lane

Ash Lane

Wookey Hole to Wells

Quarter Mile

Blue

School

Footbridge

WELLS

Parking

Cathedral Precinct

10 Wookey Hole to Wells

Distance:	2.25 miles (3.6 kms)
Maps:	Opposite & OS Explorer 141
Map Reference:	532477
Going:	An uphill walk to Arthur's Point and then downhill to level out before the final descent into Wells.

The West Mendip Way now faces three diversions on this section from the original way-marked route. However, whilst I have described the new official way in the text, in italics as usual, I have left the drawings almost as they were originally because of the historical interest described.

At the bottom of School Hill turn left up the path with the bus shelter and then the hedge on the right.

There are some small discs in this area indicating the 610 miles route of the Monarch's Way, from Worcester to Shoreham.

Go through the kissing gate, cross the stone stile and keep the hedge on the right. Keep ahead to join a developing track to the left of the houses and then bear towards the right to the gate at Milton Lane. Turn right to the village again, to the road junction.

If walking through the village from School Hill, the church and then the inn are on the left. Almost opposite is Myrtle Cottage where, in the mid-19th century, stood a cider house and orchard belonging to the inn. The former mill manager's house on the left, known as the Chilterns and now divided into three cottages, was built in the latter part of the 18th century. Opposite the village club is the post office, reputed to have been built during the reign of Queen Anne in the early 18th century.

George Savage, a Methodist minister, originally held the first religious meetings in the village in his cottage, now known as Chapel House. The first chapel to be built was in 1852 but the present building on the same site, on the left, was completed 20 years later. Chesham House, on the corner of Milton Lane, was built in 1875 and a former post office.

The West Mendip Way continues from this bend in Wells Road and through the wicket gate on the left. Keep straight ahead and up the hill, keeping the hedge close to the right, and ascend to the corner of this steeply sloping field. Pass through the gate and directly after the next gate turn left just before the lane. Climb the steep hill.

The view is of the modern suburbs of Wells with Launcherley Hill beyond. The factory in the foreground, a research establishment that produces electronic equipment, was a prisoner of war camp and some original buildings are still used. A little to the right but further afield is Hay Hill, said to be the mound of earth from the excavations for Wells Cathedral.

Keep climbing and where the stile leads into the woods pass this and keep going uphill.

Arthur's Point, at the brow of the hill, is reputed to be a lookout used by King Arthur, and it can be imagined that he did indeed stand here surveying the area around. Whether he also plotted the destruction of the Witch of Wookey as early as the 6th century can be left to the imagination as no facts supporting this have yet been presented. With Wookey Hole village in the hollow to the left, turn to face across the valley: the largest and closest farm is Lower Milton. Just beyond the barns to the left and alongside Milton Lane at the north-north-west direction is the farmhouse of Myrtle Farm. This was built in the first year of the reign of King William III, and the date of 1689 is proudly displayed.

Descend through the woods and cross the stile.

St. Cuthbert's paper mill can be seen clearly ahead with Ben Knowle Hill behind and slightly to the left.

Turn left in the field to the gate.

At the track is the entrance to the abandoned quarry of Milton Hill, its steep wall a favourite venue for climbers and cavers practising rope descents. The quarry and the three lime kilns were last used in about 1948.

Underwood Quarry and Milton Hill.

There are now two short and easy diversions that take the walker away from the quarry face of Underwood Quarry and the first is to the left, by the side of the third lime kiln. On re-joining the track after the stile, bear to the left again to follow the path. On reaching the next track, turn right and follow the lane ahead and pass the quarry on the right.

(The original route of the West Mendip Way is still a right of way and continues along the track.)

Underwood quarry becomes evident on the right with its high vertical face behind a tall wire fence. An exciting glimpse of the west front of Wells Cathedral proves that the footpath is nearing its finish.

In 1895 the quarry owners barricaded this public right of way to blast further into Milton Hill. Accompanied by the Wells town band, an angry crowd marched along here and smashed down all the barriers. Because of protests this route has since remained open for access. The quarry closed down in 1984.

Follow the quarry's perimeter and after a short distance along the tarmaced Milton Lane, bear away from it to the right, with the view of Wells directly ahead. Cross the stile close to the boundary of the nearby house. Follow the narrow descending tarmac path, which offers shade on a sunny day and cross the road. At the next road, Ash Lane, turn left and immediately right and continue ahead to enter the administration area of the Blue School.

The school was first established in 1656 in the chapel of Bubwith almshouse in Chamberlain Street to provide free education for the poor children of Wells. It was then known as the Free School of Margaret Barkham. Because of further bequests and legacies the school expanded to St. Andrew's Lodge in North Liberty in 1723. It became known as the Blue

School in about 1750 because of the free blue uniforms. The buildings to the right of the footpath were erected in 1959; those on the left were formerly the Grammar School that moved to this site in 1965. The two schools became united in 1970 under the comprehensive system.

Continue ahead through the school's playing fields.

To the right you will see the 122 feet (37 metres) high magnificent 15th century tower of St. Cuthbert's Church. The largest parish church in Somerset, this is often mistaken for the cathedral. Its beauty is enhanced by the architecture of the perpendicular period for which Somerset is well-known.

Bear left along Lover's Walk. At the next junction a small gazebo is perched high up on the wall to the right. Turn right again soon after and then left to New Street (A39) and to the eastern termination of this memorable West Mendip Way, again signified by a commemorative plaque.

To reach the cathedral precinct via the Market Place and shops, turn right along New Street with its fine 18th century town houses. Keep straight ahead at the junctions with North Liberty and Chamberlain Street and continue along Sadler Street. Opposite the 15th century White Hart Hotel is the 14th century great west gate. This, the oldest section of the Ancient Gatehouse Hotel, has a four-poster bed from Arundel Castle in the room above. Here, the ghost of a young woman dressed in a white flowing robe has been seen by staff and guests.

At the corner of High Street and the Market Place is a fountain, erected in 1799. This replaced a conduit built by Bishop Thomas de Beckyngton in the mid-15th century to direct pure drinking water from St. Andrew's springs in the Bishop's Palace grounds to the local citizens. It is from this source, or wells, that the city takes its name. The water running along the High Street gutters is an overflow from the fountain.

Vicar's Close in Wells, a mediaeval street of 1348.

Chain Gate, linking Vicar's Hall and the Cathedral in Wells.

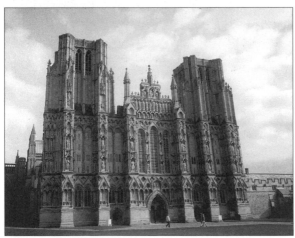

The magnificent West Front of Wells Cathedral with nearly 300 statues lodged in its many niches.

The Crown Hotel on the right of the Market Place is a 17th century coaching inn on a mid-15th century site. From one of the upper windows the Quaker William Penn, founder of Pennsylvania, preached to an assembled crowd in 1685. He was arrested and threatened with deportation but was released on the intervention of Bishop Kidder. To the right of the gatehouse, known as the Bishop's Eye, is the post office, formerly the Market Hall built in 1835. On the left-hand side by the 15th century shops is a series of marked paving slabs commemorating the long jump gold medal won by Mary Rand, a native of Wells, in the 1964 Olympic Games in Tokyo. Penniless Porch is another of Bishop Beckyngton's additions where beggars used to gather to receive alms.

The houses on the north side of Cathedral Green are mostly of 14th or 15th century foundation and have been canonical houses belonging to the Dean and Chapter of Wells for the dignitaries of Wells Cathedral. The Old Deanery, which has been rebuilt and enlarged over the centuries, was not necessarily the Dean's residence but probably his office. The Wells Museum, or Chancellor's house, is Tudor with an 18th century exterior. Although the occupants of an earlier medieval canonical house did hold the office of Chancellor, the present building was not used officially as the Chancellor's home. Mr. W.S. Hodgkinson, who bought Wookey Hole paper mill in 1848, was one of the tenants here for a few years up to 1874.

The museum was founded in 1893 by Henry Ernest Balch who was born in Wells in 1869. He was the greatest of Mendip archaeologists and pioneered the exploration of Swildon's Hole and Eastwater Cavern at Priddy, and also excavated Wookey Hole in 1904. The museum originally occupied rooms above the west cloister in the cathedral but moved to this present building in 1930.

The building next door, opposite the north porch of the cathedral, was once known as the Archdeacon's House as many of the tenants since the 14th century have held this title. It has been rebuilt over the centuries and it became an assembly and banqueting room from 1769. After 1800 it was one of many small breweries then in Wells, called the Old City Brewery, and after about 1880 it belonged to the Wells Theological College. It is now used as the music section of the Wells Cathedral School. This school, established in the 13th century, is one of the oldest in the country; rooms over the cathedral's west cloister were still used up to the 19th century. This school now occupies most of the other and older buildings in nearby Liberty.

Vicar's Close is a mediaeval street of 42 cells, or houses, which date from 1348 and is claimed to be the oldest continuously inhabited street in Europe. The Chain Gate over the road gives a covered way from the Vicar's Hall to the north transept of the cathedral.

A church was founded here by King Ina and St. Aldhelm in 707 AD but this was replaced by another in about 1180 which grew over the next 150 years into the triumphant splendour of St. Andrew's Cathedral. The glorious west front, with nearly 300 statues, is a unique addition of about 1230; the central tower was built in 1318 and the other two towers were erected separately with the second being completed in 1424. The original 14th century clock with its revolving mechanical figures has been much renewed since this date and can be seen on the wall in the north transept. (The face on the exterior is of the 19th century.) The amazing scissor arches were constructed in about 1348.

The early 13th century Bishop's Palace is the rarest in England. The fortifications, gatehouse and drawbridge were added in the 14th century and since that time the palace has been renovated and enlarged but still retains a mediaeval style. St. Andrew's wells feed the moat and the famous swans can occasionally be seen ringing the bell below the window on the side of the gatehouse for food.

Wells became a city by a royal charter granted by King John in 1201 and it has since grown into a truly beautiful but bustling market town. A visit in November can be highlighted by the exciting floodlit carnival procession of more than 100 floats with their active or static displays, just one of many similar carnivals in the area during this month.

As a touring centre for the Mendip Hills area of Somerset, Wells is ideally situated and it is indeed unique and one of the most charming and impressive of our cathedral cities.

Accommodation is plentiful but camping and caravanning facilities are not found in the city. The tourist information office, situated at the side of the Georgian Town Hall of 1779 in Market Place, offers friendly advice and local guidebooks.

Penniless Porch in Wells Market Square.